General Principles
of
The Kabbalah

ברכה בריאות הצלחה אושר ועושר

חיים טובים וארוכים למשפחת טהרני

מתתיהו בן עמרם ומרים

שהין בת נאמת ומולוד ספאי

והילדים

דוד (Siamak) בן מתתיהו

שיבא בת מתתיהו

שיזכו לנישואין עם בני זוגם האמתיים בקרוב

ברכה והצלחה

סוזן בת מתתיהו

ובעלה

מיכאל בן סיני לוי

אביו

סיני בן חביב לוי

לחיים ארוכים ובריאות

מולוד בת אריסטו

לעילוי נשמת

עמרם בן משה טהרני ז"ל

מרים בת אברהם טהרני ז"ל

נאמת בן אהרון ז"ל

הרצל בן נאמת ז"ל

לאה בת אקדס ומאיר סיאני ז"ל

General Principles

of

The Kabbalah

by

RABBI MOSES C. LUZZATTO

Translation by
DR. PHILIP S. BERG

Research Centre of Kabbalah
Jerusalem — New York

First Edition - August 1970
Second Edition - February 1984
Third Edition - December 1988

ISBN 0-943688-07-8 (Hardcover)
0-943688-31-0 (Softcover)

For further information, address:
RESEARCH CENTRE OF KABBALAH
200 PARK AVENUE, Suite 303 East
NEW YORK, N.Y. 10017

— OR —

RESEARCH CENTRE OF KABBALAH
P.O. BOX 14168
THE OLD CITY, JERUSALEM
ISRAEL

PRINTED IN U.S.A.
1988

CONTENTS

CONTENTS

CONTENTS

Research Center Books of Related Interest
Ask your bookseller for the books you have missed

ENTRANCE TO THE ZOHAR, compiled and edited by Dr. Philip S. Berg
ENTRANCE TO THE TREE OF LIFE, compiled and edited by Dr. Philip S. Berg
REINCARNATION: THE WHEELS OF A SOUL, by Dr. Philip S. Berg (also edited in Hebrew, Spanish and French)
KABBALAH FOR THE LAYMAN I, by Dr. Philip S. Berg (also edited in Hebrew, Spanish, French, Russian and German)
KABBALAH FOR THE LAYMAN II, by Dr. Philip S.Berg
KABBALAH FOR THE LAYMAN III, by Dr. Philip S.Berg
TEN LUMINOUS EMANATIONS, vol. 1, compiled and edited by R. Levi Krakovsky
TEN LUMINOUS EMANATIONS, vol. 2, compiled and edited by Dr. Philip S. Berg
LIGHT OF REDEMPTION, by R. Levi Krakovsky
GENERAL PRINCIPLES OF KABBALAH, by R.M. Luzatto
THE KABBALAH CONNECTION, by Dr. Philip S. Berg
ASTROLOGY, THE STAR CONNECTION, by Dr. Philip S. Berg (also edited in Hebrew, Spanish and French)
ZOHAR: PARASHAT PINHAS, vols.1, 2 and 3 translated and edited by Dr. Philip Berg
POWER OF THE ALEPH BETH, vols. 1 and 2 by Dr. Philip S. Berg
KABBALAH FOR BEGINNERS, by Karen Berg(in cassete tapes)

BOOKS IN PRINT

KABBALISTIC MEDITATION, by Dr. Philip S. Berg
ASTROLOGY: ECHO OF THE FUTURE, by Dr. Philip S. Berg
TEN LUMINOUS EMANATIONS, vol.3 compiled and edited by Dr. Philip S. Berg

PREFACE

I

The present spiritual revival has been phenomenal. But, unfortunately, with it have not come the answers to the demanding questions that have been raised. Naturally, an endless amount of print has been devoted to some of the most obvious and simple questions that man has been asking of himself, but to no avail. The intent of this preface, therefore, is to demonstrate how the Kabbalah can solve man's perplexities.

What we can attempt through study of the Kabbalah is to conclusively prove, via *cause and effect,* that behind everything lies a motivating cause, the effect of which must inevitably follow. And in attempting this the Kabbalah makes various assumptions which, if within the entire universe there is no room for contradiction, we then must assume to be correct.

The inability at times to understand the unseen cause is neither detrimental in evaluating a given situation, nor is this concern for not understanding the unseen cause. For example, in a theatre where one thousand people are observing a bottle on the table, everyone is told to leave.

After the theatre has been totally emptied, all entrances are then sealed from the outside. Several moments later the audience re-enters the theatre, only to observe the bottle now resting on a chandelier. Although everyone is certain that nobody entered to remove the bottle from the table, no one will assume that the bottle reached its destination by itself. The reason for this is that the bottle is included in the phase of effect, and not in the cause, since a bottle can not motivate or cause anything. Therefore, we can make the assumption that someone *caused* the bottle to be moved, although the cause has neither been determined nor seen. In other words, our assumptions will be *true* causes of the effects around us; they will withstand the makings of our universe, and not fall prey to our symptomatic way of understanding through relativity.

As another example the *cause* or reason of narcotic addiction was formerly held to be poverty. How was this conclusion arrived at? Merely by observing a given situation or effect. For in the absence of a better reason, we latch on to what appears to be a justifiable cause so as to satisfy a substantial amount of the effects. What we have conclusively failed to provide, however, is whether this cause satisfies each and every situation relating to narcotic addiction—which it hasn't. It is then apparent that poverty has not been the true cause or reason, for narcotic addiction has also been rampant among the affluent. Thus, we must look again for the true cause.

True cause must be able to withstand tomorrow's events. For who can be so bold as to make predictions when one has not tasted or experienced the events of the future? It is truly to sneer at those who, with their limitations of time, space and motion, advance their theories of tomorrow, based solely on present environmental existence; for the future, with its inevitable contradiction of events will disprove all these limited theories. Still, in the absence of any other method of forecasting future developments, our economists, scientists and ecologists must use this limited form of reasoning to provide an answer for the majority of present and future events. However, we must recognize that the word "cause" is being misused, since cause is the direct motivating force behind every effect. And if we mistake the true nature of cause, we will not have faced future effects and events with reality.

Our scientists glow with their technological advancements. And rightfully so, for a great deal of labor, time and money has gone into producing these advancements, which we shall assume have enhanced our lives. Yet (and in no way is the following statement to demean these advances), all that the scientist has done is merely discover something that already exists; that is, he has observed a reaction, but without knowing the true cause of this reaction. We may therefore conclude that, to some extent, the troubled times we are experiencing today can be directly related to the see-sawing events of cause and effect. Yet the cause advanced yesterday will not hold up tomorrow. This inevitably must create confusion, in which we are caught up in all kinds of theories which, however, are not the true answers. And despite these scientific advances, where just the understanding of

effect takes precedence, we must remain in constant
fear of what this effect will bring tomorrow.

Our previous illustration of narcotic addiction
(chosen because of its serious implication and effects on
society) is classic. Two answers advanced as to why the
widspread use of drugs are their availability and today's
troubled times. These two causes, however, only give an
insight to our convenient, symptomatic reasoning. For
drugs have been known to mankind since time immemo-
rial, and have always been available to the young and old
alike. And needless to say we have had troubled times
since the recording of history. Yet so-called qualified
thinkers of our day will advance such apparently immature reasoning, believing that these are the causes.
But a true cause will have to avoid direct contradiction
for it to be truly classified as the "cause". There is
a cause, but it will have to withstand some very severe
testing and constant questioning, paying heed to the
limiting factors of time, space and motion.

Still another example, is the medical researcher. He
discovered that penicillin destroys streptococcus, yet
without knowing why. The fact is that only through
the application of relativity is he certain that penicillin
works. He can only observe the effect; that is, the
blackened area where the streptococcus is being destroyed. This is the extent of his observation, for he still lacks
the true cause. This does not mean that the scientist does
not have a desire to know and understand the cause.
But he must be careful in attempting to arrive at some
definitive cause, for his cause must justify every aspect
of the workings of penicillin. In other words, he has

not explained why the reaction to the drug is not the same in all cases.

From the preceding we can conclude that (1) at times we accept a cause although it is unseen, and (2) even where it is quite apparent that the given cause will not hold up in every instance of its effect, still, if in the majority of cases it is plausible, it is acceptable. This then is where the Kabbalah offers a definite insight as to the true cause, which inevitably leads to the truth of cause and effect. Thus, from the causal assumption of the Kabbalah we will have discovered a definite pattern, thereby convincing us of an omniscient Creator.

Let us now outline some of the questions man has been asking of himself:

1. What is our existence all about?

2. What is our purpose in this endless chain of creation where we appear to be the least important, as compared to the wondrous worlds of the universe?

3. Self-reflection can only reveal to us our imperfections. Yet, how is this possible, seeing that we have been created by the Holy One, Whose perfect agency must necessarily produce perfect works?

4. One of the accepted assumptions of religious belief is that the Creator is All Good; therefore His intention must be to do all that is good. Why, then, did he create beings whose entire existence is one of endless pain and misery?

5. How, then, is it possible that there should spring forth from the Eternal, which has neither beginning nor end, but considered infinite, finite and temporary beings, who are doomed to death and destruction?

6. Why is the earth round? Why does the moon have no light of its own, but reflecting, instead, the light of the sun? Why is the satellite Telstar round? Why must the eye contain four colors, with the black segment (the pupil) of the eye serving as the receiving instrument? Why ten fingers and not nine or eleven? In other words, why is any part of this universe created as it is? Is there a set pattern? What does this pattern signifify? What does it mean for man?

7. The widespread interest in the occult suddenly appears to have taken a firm hold on a great majority of people in general, and countless Jews in particular. Why now? Do the occult religions answer all of the questions that one may ask of his surroundings? In fact many, if not all, of these occult religions refer to the Kabbalah as their origin or course; then why not the study of the Kabbalah? If in essence the Kabbalah is total Truth, it must embody all of the studies known to man, such as: Biology, Philosophy, Zoology, Astrology, Astronomy, Medicine and so on. Then why not study the source?

To make all this wholly clear, we must first engage in certain inquiries. Not where it is forbidden, namely regarding the Creator's substantiality—for no thought can encompass Him at all, therefore there being no way in which we can think or speak about Him; but where we are commanded to inquire, namely regarding his deeds, as the Torah instructs: "Know thy father's God and serve Him".

The first inquiry concerns the question of how the creation can be conceived as being "new" in the sense that something was not contained in the Holy One before He created it. This should be clear to anyone capable of logical thought since there is nothing that is not contained in Him. For can anyone give what is not within him?

The second inquiry concerns this: being omnipotent the Creator can certainly create something from nothing; that is, something that had no existence in Him in any way. Then what is this existence, of which it can be said to have no place within Him, but that which is new.

The third inquiry concerns what the Masters of the Kabbalah have said: that man's soul is part of God on high. This means that there is no difference between Him and the soul, except that He is "the whole" and the Soul is "part". The sages' metaphor for this is a stone hewn from a mountain, there being no difference between the stone and the mountain, save for the one being "part" and the other "the whole". Now we can envisage a stone being separated from the mountain by a suitable tool, by which the "part" is separated

from the "whole". But how can we envisage the Holy
One, separating a part of His substantiality, which, in
turn, becomes a "part" (the Soul) so distinct from it,
that it can then be conceived as being only a part of His
substantiality?

The fourth inquiry is: since the chariot of the
Other Side (Evil Forces) and the Husks are so utterly
remote from His Holiness that we cannot envisage the
distance, how is it possible that it should proceed from,
and be brought forth, by His Holiness? Furthermore,
why is it that His Holiness should even keep it in
existence?

The fifth inquiry concerns the Resurrection of the
Dead. Since the body is such a contemptible thing,
being condemned to die and be buried from the very
moment of its birth (the Zohar even says that as long
as the body is not entirely decomposed and something
of it still remains, the soul cannot ascend to its place
in Paradise), therefore, why is it necessary that it
should arise again at the Resurrection of the Dead?
Can the Holy One not give pleasure to the soul without
it? And even stranger is the saying of our Sages: "The
dead will come to life again with all their infirmities,
lest it be said that they are not the same, and then
the Holy One will heal their infirmities." We want
to understand why it should matter to the Holy One
that it might be said that they are different, to the
extent that He should have to create their infirmities
again and then have to heal them.

The subject of our sixth inquiry is what our Sages
have said: that man is the center of all existence, and

that all the Upper Worlds and this material World have been created only for him. Zohar Wayikra No. 48, The Sages also require man to believe that the World has been created for him (Sanhdrin No. 37). On the face of it, it is hard to understand that for this little man, who does not account for as much as a hair's worth in the existence of this World, the Holy One should have created all this. Also, why does man need all this?

If we are to understand all these questions and inquiries, we must first consider the purpose of Creation. Nothing can be understood while it is being made, but only after it is completed. And it is clear that there can be no maker without purpose, for only someone whose mind is unbalanced works without any purpose.

Now I know full well that there are would-be scholars (who have thrown off the' yoke of the Torah and its Commandments), who say that the Creator created the world and then abandoned it to its fate. The reason for this, they say, is that because of the worthlessness of all creatures, it does not befit the Creator, in all His Exaltedness, to watch their despicable ways. But that argument is invalid; for we cannot decide that we are base and worthless unless we decide that we have made ourselves (and all that is naturally corrupt and despicable in us). However, when we decide that the Creator, in His Supreme Perfection, is the artisan who created and designed our bodies, with all the good and evil inclinations inherent in them, it follows then that the perfect Maker can never be said to have turned out despicable, corrupt work, for every action testifies to its own quality.

Is it the fault of a ruined coat if it had been sewn by an inept tailor? This idea is corroborated in Tractate Taanith (20), thus: "Once Rabbi Eliezer, son of Rabbi Shimon, happened to meet a man who was extremely ugly and said to him, 'How ugly is this man'. Whereupon the ugly man replied: "Go say to the artisan who made me: How ugly is this vessel which you have made."

Thus, those would-be scholars, who say that because of our baseness and worthlessness it does not befit the Almighty to watch over us and that He has abandoned us, merely proclaim their own ignorance. Imagine meeting someone to whom it had occurred to create creatures, intended from the first to be plagued and suffer like us, while being left to their own devices without any assistance whatsoever. How deeply would you blame and despise him! Is it then conceivable that this would apply to the Holy One, Blessed and Praised Be He?

Therefore, common sense demands that we understand matters as being the opposite of what they seem to be. We must decide that we are, in truth, such excellent and exalted creatures that there is no limit to our importance and, therefore, befitting the artisan who made us. For whatever shortcomings of the body seems to possess they only fall back on the Creator who made us with all that is in us by nature. It is obvious that He has made us and not we ourselves; that He also knew all the consequences that would continue to result from all the natural and evil inclinations which he implanted in us. But here, as we have said, we must look to the purpose of the matter, so as to be able to understand. Thus, this is revealed in the proverb, "Do not show a fool a job half done."

Our Sages have taught us (see Etz Hayim, Chapter of the vessels, 81) that the Holy One has created the world for the purpose of giving enjoyment to those whom He has created. This is what we must attend to with all our thoughts, for this is the purpose of the Creation of the World. Consider this: since the Thought of Creation was to give enjoyment to His creatures, it follows that He created within the Souls an extremely great measure of the "will to receive" what he thought to give them. For the dimension of any pleasure or enjoyment is measured by the dimension of the "will to receive" it. In other words, the greater the "will to receive," the greater the pleasure; the less the "will to receive," the less the pleasure taken in receiving. Hence, the very Thought of Creation requires that the Creation within the soul of the "will to receive" be in exceedingly great measure, for the great enjoyment and the great will to receive are commensurate.

Having learned this, we should then achieve a clear understanding of our second inquiry, regarding the Creation of that which did not exist within the substantiality of the omnipotent Holy One. It follows then that God's thought of Creation, which is to give enjoyment to His creatures, did of necessity create the "will to receive" His good intentions. Thus, we understand that this "will to receive" could certainly *not* have been contained within His substantiality, for from whom could He have received? Therefore, He created something new that was not within Him. At the same time, it is clear from the Thought of the Creation that there was no need whatsover to create anything *beyond* this "will to receive"; for this new Creation was, in itself, the sufficient means through which the Almighty would bestow His enjoyment to us.

All that is supplementary in the Thought of Creation, namely all manner of benefits which He conceived for us, proceeds in direct procession from the substantiality of the Holy One. Thus, there is no reason for Him to create the benefits anew, since they already proceed, as something made from something else, to the great "will to receive" that is within the soul. Therefore, it should be understood that the essential matter in the new Creation, from beginning to end, is the "will to receive".

It is this "will to receive," which, through a continuous evolvement, dominates our physical universe, and causes the multitude of different characteristics and manifestations of development. In other words, there is nothing in our existence that does not stem from the "will to receive."

We may notice, for example, an individual who eats very little, or another who eats a great deal. It would be inaccurate to conclude that the individual with a hearty appetite would have to be fat, or that the one with a lesser appetite be thin. The one who eats a great deal would be considered to have a greater desire for food, while the one eating little is said to have a lesser desire for food. Consequently, the physical makeup has no bearing on the desires of the individual, since they are separate and distinct.

The Kabbalah states that when this new phenomenon "will to receive" was created, it required four specific phases to be initiated. Let us use an illustration to comprehend the necessity of the Four Phases.

If I were the Creator and had a desire to impart some benevolence, the mere fact that I inserted this "goodie" in one's pocket would not necessarily carry with it the effect of one's wanting the "goodie". There would first have to be a desire on the part of the recipient to want this object, although from the giver's standpoint, there was an imparting. Thus, phase One, where the desire to receive was inevitably created to satisfy the desire of the Creator to impart, certainly could not be considered as having a true desire to receive. Also, phase One by receiving this benevolence from the creator, or imparter, inevitably received the characteristic of imparting, included within the benevolence.

Phase Two came about when the "desire to receive" felt a desire to impart as well. When this occurred, the benevolence removed itself from the recipient, thereby creating phase Three. This phase is void of any coercive means, coercion of receiving could not indicate an imparting aspect.

Now, when benevolence removed itself, the desire to receive felt a true lack of this benevolence thus causing a *Real* desire to receive which it lacked. This *Real* desire, then, is considered as phase Four.

These four phases were considered within the very first stage of Creation, meaning "The Endless World," where the desire to receive, manifested as a pure Light, received endlessly from the desire to *impart*.

At this point, the Kabbalah relates that nothing was lacking, except for the defect experienced by the desire to receive. The Zohar terms this defect whereby the receiver receives constantly without ever benefiting the imparter or giver, as the "Bread of shame". From our experience we know that the constant receiver will eventually begin to resent the hand that feeds him. Now, knowing well that it was the intent of the Creator to impart, the receiver (desire to receive) refused to receive, unless he could reciprocate; for the inevitability of receiving could never be effaced or destroyed, but would have to remain, since this was the reason of Creation.

Thus, through a series of endless changes in the desire to receive, the final manifestation of this desire to receive was the formation of man epitomized by greed. Here is where man would have the opportunity of receiving and still impart delight (by his acceptance) to the Creator.

Let us assume that one is to receive a fortune of money, which would naturally be welcomed as a result of one's desire to receive. But because of man's ability to control and master his own Destiny he refuses to accept purely for the sake of receiving. He then considers this fortunate opportunity as a way to benefit mankind, in that he, in turn, could bestow this wealth upon others. And for this very reason he would accept.

This then is the thought man must have before he can receive: knowing well that the Creator delights in one's acceptance, even though there is the chance of refusal which would be contrary to the Creator's intent, and by accepting on the basis of imparting, the recipient does not feel the "bread of shame". The following analogy clearly illustrates the preceding thought.

A wealthy man in town is about to sit down to a sumptuous meal. Suddenly, peering through a window, he observes a man in rags who obviously has not had a decent meal in days. The rich man invites the poor man in and requests that he partake in the meal. The poor man refuses gently, indicating that he really doesn't need the assistance of the wealthy benefactor. Knowing well that the poor man is in need of a meal and having a desire to do good, he repeatedly insists that the poor man accept his offer. The poor man, although desirous of this meal, refuses because of an innate feeling of "bread of shame." After numerous requests the poor man finally agrees, thereby causing tremendous delight to the wealthy man.

Now what has actually happened here? The wealthy man, the benefactor suddenly feels he is on the receiving end, and the poor man becomes the imparter, giving delight to the benefactor. We begin to sense a *circular feeling* running between benefactor and recipient; that is, in receiving there is imparting (the poor man), and with imparting there is receiving (the rich man). This is the cardinal rule of the Kabbalah for one's receiving in any manner or form. In other words, provided there is an element of imparting with the receiving, the receiving is unlimited.

If however, receiving is merely for oneself, then there is a limit the vessel (the body) may receive, just as a cup limits its contents to the brim of the vessel. But were we to imagine the cup receiving from the outside while imparting simultaneously then there would be limitless receiving.

Essentially, this is the reason of our being: to receive the benevolence of the Creator, but without the element of greed. Therefore, we must condition ourselves so that the Inner Light will have sway over the body (desire to receive). Therefore, we must remove the limitation of the body, which is, in essence, the factor governing our very existence.

Thre are three basic governing limitations: time, space and motion. However, within the metaphysical realm, these three components do not exist. How then, can we possibly comprehend metaphysical matters?

The Kabbalah compares a person to a tree in a field, with the tree and its root corresponding to man and his origin. From this we can make important deductions.

We know that a tree is comprised of a root, trunk, branches and fruit, all of which emanate from the root. However, the root shows no sign of its· future, whereby it develops into a tree. Although within the seed of the tree all future manifestations must exist, nevertheless, we as human beings cannot discern their varying future developments. Why? Because the body is composed of the limiting factor of time, space and motion. Thus, as the seed develops in time, space and motion, we visually experience the development. But the limitations need not govern.

Let us take time as a factor. We have all experienced days that either drag or pass swiftly by. How do we explain this? Is time 24 hours in a day?

Let us assume that a man has been placed in a dungeon for a week's time. When he is freed he has absolutely no conception of either what time of the day it is, or how many days have gone by. It is apparent that time is not a governing factor, but more like a basket in which actions are accumulated. Now, if the basket is full of useful accomplishments one feels that the day has gone by quickly. But if the reverse were true, that is, if the basket were empty, one would feel the weightiness of time.

The astronauts, for example, have displayed to us the dissipation of these limiting factors. If it now takes one and a half hours to traverse the earth, where the governing factor of gravity apparently has no place, then the distance in the future will suddenly become nonexistent—almost to the point of being in two places at the same time! Therefore, it may not require any time or motion to move from one place to another; all will occur almost simultaneously, although, presently, we still cannot discern different concepts contained within one.

We may clarify the problem by examining the finality of an act, which is present in the first contemplation or thought of that act. This principle applies not only to the thought of Creation, but also to man's thoughts. A multitude of thoughts may go into the accomplishment of any act, yet in the very first thought of an act—its finality is already present.

For example, in planning a house, the first thought is the picture of the complete structure. However, before this is achieved, many details need to be thought out and acted upon. The finished house follows only after many thoughts and many actions. Thus we say that the final act is present in the first thought.

We are taught the simple, fundamental idea that by thought of God alone, everything was created and brought to its completion. God, however, is not like man, for man must utilize real tools and devices in order for his acts and plans to be materialized. But God's thought, by itself, suffices to complete all acts instantly.

With the concept whereby the body or the limiting factor need not have sway over the Light or Soul, we can now account for E. S. P., and why it may work between two individuals.

As has been explained, the divisive factor between two souls is the "will to receive." It then follows that, were this factor to be diminished or transmuted to one of imparting, the two individuals may communicate with each other without the aid of any physical means; for we have demonstrated that time, space and motion are the limiting factors, provided the body still holds sway over the Light or Soul.

As another example, a physical wall separating two rooms remains as a limiting factor only for those governed by physical elements. Everything existing within Creation is but a photo-copy of some form of the "will to receive." Were the particular aspect consisting of the dividing wall removed (metaphysically speaking) the wall would no longer remain as a limiting factor.

With new scientific advances constantly appearing on the scene, the metaphysical concept can be understood. If one had stated some 50 years ago that the noted Kabbalist, Rabbi Isaac Luria, could travel from Safed to Jerusalem within a matter of seconds, there would be little understanding of this seemingly wild statement today, however, this can be understood as being possible—if one understands the metaphysical concept.

Furthermore, with a clearer conception of what consists of cause and effect, we may comprehend that the author of the Kabbalah (the Zohar) Rabbi Shimon Ben Yohai, did, in fact, know the *exact* reason (as opposed to the result of trial and error) why a particular herb would react in a given situation.

Now to the misery and suffering that we all experience in one form or another. This does not (and could not) emanate from the Creator, since He is All Good. From whence does it come? Indirectly, for actions and occurrences are *Good*, but due to *our* inabilities of time, space and motion, they appear to be bad.

Take, for example, the individual who is to conclude a very successful business deal in some distant city and must arrive there with a check at a specific time. For some unknown reason his watch stopped, and upon arrival at the airport, he is told that his plane has just left. Can one imagine the unhappiness and disappointment experienced by this individual? But this condition is short-lived, for upon leaving the airport in his car he tunes in some music on the radio to cheer up his spirits—when suddenly a bulletin comes across the airwaves announcing the crash of the very airplane he was scheduled to be on! No survivors! His mood immediately changes, from feeling distraught to one of relief, if not overjoyed.

Now how is this possible with the same situation to experience such greatly divergent moods? It is, however, quite obvious that, due to his inability to rise above the limiting factor called time, he could not have visualized the next few moments in time.

It is therefore quite apparent that the governing elements of a "desire to receive" (the "I" and the "Me") are actually the responsible causes of both happiness and unhappiness. Thus, it is this "will to receive" that is the root of all misery and suffering.

Why is the earth round? To clearly indicate to man his reason for existence, and the reason of his essential being.* Man must transmute his "will to receive" to one of imparting so as to create the circular concept whereby giving or imparting enables one to receive endlessly and satisfactorily.

Why is the moon black when not reflecting the light it receives from the sun, and thereby demonstrating to man his makeup? Black represents the epitome

---

* See page 15 for circular concept.

of greed, for it has no light of its own. This means that it can *only* receive before imparting.

Man is constantly engaged in the battle of the pure ("will to impart") verses the impure ("will to receive"). Within all Creation, wherever we may find the concept of evil, therein lies the manifestation of goodness. There is no element within Creation that does not contain these two basic elements, whether it be an electric current with its positive (imparting) and negative (receiving) charges or the atom.

Therefore, the scientist, without the available Kabbalah knowledge, constructed the Telstar satellite in a circular form via trial and error. Telstar * because of its receiving messages from without and as a circular ** object (indicating the element of imparting), therefore receives and emits endlessly. This is what we call root information or causative-motivation.

From the preceding, the reason why one possesses a left and right hand becomes obvious, as well as why each hand has five fingers: to indicate the four varying degrees of the "will to receive" with its pure and impure source. Therefore, each individual's right hand is somewhat longer, in the hope that his right "will to impart" will extend over his left ("will to receive").

The reason why the eye has four different colors, with the pupil always being black, is to also show the

---

* *In a triangular or squared type of construction Telstar could not be effective.*

** *It is strange to find that the Hebrew word "Sephira" is translated in English as "Sphere".*

four varying degrees of the "will to receive". The pupil, which serves as the actual vessel of receiving, is black because it lacks the ability to impart.

And why is the drug scene prevalent now? The Kabbalah states that in the time of the Messiah (also known as the "age of Aquarius") there will occur a tremendous spiritual awakening, the cause of which is the violent revolt of the soul against the governing limitations of the body. For the soul will have had its fill. And the senseless crushing effect of the "I" (will to receive) will be displaced by the love of one's neighbor and consideration for one's friend. This is the root cause for today's "Love" movements; this too is the motivating factor for the drug scene *now*.

The inner depths of man, call it the subconscious if you will, have been stirred up. Man wants to *get away* from the insatiable "desire to receive" for oneself, and from the clutches of our limiting factors. For drugs do simulate this experience; one *does* become oblivious to his physical surroundings.

However, one thing is wrong. On the return to his present surroundings the individual is back to where he started from. Returning too are his fears, frustrations and inabilities all of which stem from the causative factor, the body ("will to receive"). This is not symptomatic reasoning, changing with time or weather conditions. It may, however, be irrational, but it is not illogical.

Must this violent revolt of the soul manifest itself within our society? Must we experience the violence on campus, conflict throughout the world? Or is there some logical method to tame man's self-destructive madness?

This is where the educational process of the Kabbalah will contribute. It is the long sought after conditioning agent that will lead man from his own concerned way of life to recognizing his purpose in being.

DR. PHILIP S. BERG

INTRODUCTION

Thirteen years in a cave . . . a father and son alone . . . and the *ZOHAR* took form—the "Book of Splendor", the classic work on the Torah's hidden lore and mysticism.

When Rome ruled Israel, Rabbi Shimon ben Yohai was a disciple of Rabbi Akiva, who had taught Torah despite the persecution of the Romans, till they put him to death. Rabbi Shimon lashed out at the Romans for their evil and cruelty—and Rome sentenced him to death.

Telling no one, he fled with his son Rabbi El'azar to a cave amid the mountains of Israel. They hid there, thirteen years till the Roman emperor's death made it safe for them to leave.

Since earliest times there were secret teachings of Divine mysteries in the Torah, that could only interest a few . . . that only a few enlightened souls could understand. There were texts, mentioned in the Talmud, that originated centuries before. And the Talmud tells of Sages who worked to master such esoteric lore.

The years that Rabbi Shimon ben Yohai spent with his son in the cave, marked a turning-point in the history of this great body of hidden knowledge. In the safety of darkness, with no text to read, Rabbi Shimon drew on the deep levels of memory and vision stored in his unconscious from years of study with his masters of the past.

So the Zohar took form—a single work that became the classic text of kabbalah, the received, transmitted mystic teachings of Judaism. In every generation
afterward, a select few guarded it and studied it—until
a widespread yearning grew in 14th century Spain
for the life-giving teachings of kabbalah. Then the
Zohar became known, to be hidden no more.

Many studied and understood the dazzling truths
of Jewish mysticism. But few could make others understand and see. For that, Jewry would have to wait
for Safed in the 1500's.

In a small city in Upper Galilee, set on a hill
in a lovely mountainous region of Israel, kabbalah flourished as never before. Jews lived a simple religious life
in Safed, supporting themselves, seeking only peace and
piety.

There Rabbi Moses Cordovero' was born in 1522.
Drawn as by a thirst to the wisdom of kabbalah, he
studied with Rabbi Sh'lomo Alkabetz, author of L'cha
Dodi, whose sister he married.

In time, kabbalah found in him what it had long
needed: a gifted teacher with a pen. The few works
of his that were printed, give the clearest presentation
ever made of the main teachings of Jewish mysticism.
Through his words in print, the brilliant light of kabbalah
later reached Eastern Europe, to give dynamic life to
the great movement of hassidus.

At the same time, Safed had a second master of
kabbalah: Rabbi Isaac Luria, called the Ari.

In his teens the Ari was already a Talmudic authority. Then he discovered the Zohar, and for 13

years he lived as a hermit, plumbing its secrets. In 1569 he settled in Safed, to study briefly with Rabbi Moses Cordovero, until he became a master in his own right, with a devoted circle of disciples.

The Ari could not put his own thoughts down on paper. They were too complex—too filled with rich, interwoven images and allusions, associations and metaphors. But his disciples recorded every possible word and deed, producing the volumes of what we now regard as "his writings."

While the "writings" were now recorded, nevertheless, the subject matter was to wait till the early 1900's; when a gifted student was to reveal these "writings" intelligibly to the masses.

It started with a modern pioneer—Rabbi Judah Ashlag. A rarely gifted teacher, he could unlock doors for the very beginner, and bring new vision, new awareness in kabbalah's great truths.

As his lifetime on earth ended, Rabbi Ashlag left three legacies. The first was ha-Sulam, a 21-volume translation-commentary that renders the Zohar from its original abstruse, difficult Aramaic into clear, flowing Hebrew.

His second legacy was Talmud Eser S'firos, an essential introduction to kabbalah for the novice. No other work of this kind was ever written before.

The third legacy was his disciple, Rabbi Judah Z. Brandwein.

Rabbi Brandwein directed Yeshiva Kol Yehuda (Research Centre of Kabbalah) an academy for the study of the Torah's mysticism, founded by Rabbi Judah Ashlag 50 years ago.

With it's return to the Walled City of Jerusalem, the Research Centre of Kabbalah has flowered anew in Israel, in a new period of remarkable growth. There gifted students may learn this lore, in an unbroken tradition that prevailed during the old days of Rabbi Shimon ben Yohai.

In addition, the Research Centre of Kabbalah was founded, in the United States, to maintain the Academy in Jerusalem, and—more important—to embark on a major, unprecedented program of publications in Hebrew and English.

BIOGRAPHICAL NOTES

For a brief span of forty years, in the beginning of the eighteenth century (1707-1747), the genius of Moses Hayyim Luzzatto, kabbalist and poet, lit up the field of Hebrew learning and letters. Too soon was his life cut off when, shortly after reaching Palestine—which was then considered the only true soil for kabbalistic productions—he contracted the plague and died.

He had been born into a well-to-do family, in Padua, who were no strangers to high culture and scholarship. His father, Jacob Vita Luzzatto, gave him a fine education, such as befitted a rich young man. He was taught Latin as well as the Hebrew poets, and while still a young boy, was entered into the Talmud Torah of Padua to begin a thorough course of religious training.

Luzzatto's teacher in secular knowledge was Isaac Hayyim Cohen Cantarini, a physician and an accomplished scholar. Rabbi Isaiah Bassan was Luzzatto's religious teacher, and it was his influence that touched the young student even more deeply than did that of Cantarini. In fact, it was from Bassan's father-in-law, Rabbi Benjamin Cohen Vitali, that Luzzatto was first to learn of the Kabbalah—that which fired his imagination during his student years, up a veritable fountain of life, and remaining within him until the end of his life.

Many books concerning Kabbalah came from his pen; yet, he was highly gifted in other aspects of literary creation as well. Luzzatto has in fact been called the "father of modern Hebrew literature".

At the core of the Jewish consciousness there always lies the Messianic hope—the dream of God's Kingdom established on earth. And in Luzzatto this consciousness was so highly developed that it dominated his writings and his teachings. He wanted to kindle the "Great Light"—to walk with his students in God's own ways— and to ignite the very fires of Heaven. It was to this end that he gathered about him a group of students, and together they studied and read the divine wisdom of the Kabbalah. It cannot, however, be said that he was officially tolerated or that his work was understood for as soon as his activities became known, the Venetian rabbinate interfered. Their persecution eventually drove him from Padua to Amsterdam. For ten years Luzzatto remained in Amsterdam, where he was highly honored and revered for his great learning and erudition, as well as for his piety. It was here that he wrote one of his best-known works, *MESSILAT YESHARIM* (the Righteous Path), and here it was published in 1740.

Luzzatto's love for and interest in the Kabbalah never flagged. In 1743 he and his family migrated to the Holy Land in order that he might continue his public teaching of the Kabbalah despite the ban placed on these teachings by the Italian rabbis. Luzzatto's teacher Bassan had supported him throughout the conflict, but he had been unable to convince the rabbis of Luzzatto's sincerity and of the great merit of his work.

Little is known of the few remaining years of Luzzatto's life in Palestine. The following elegy composed by the rabbis of Tiberias in the year 1747, gives evidence, however, of his great success:

> "Hear, O Heavens, and give ear, O Earth, because the chief of rabbis, the divine Kabbalist, the Israel . . . our teacher and master, Rabbi Moses Hayyim Luzzatto died, he and all his family, of the plague . . . and is buried in Tiberias, near Rabbi Akiba's grave. Happy is he, in this world and the world to come, but woe to us, because our crown fell from off our head."

In spite of his brief and often tragic life, Rabbi Moshe Hayyim Luzzatto contributes an inportant insight into the interpretation of the *SEFIROT* without which the *ZOHAR*, or source of Kabbalah, could not be understood.

Chapter
One

It is a common place of Jewish wisdom that that
which comes to the mind first is brought into action last.
Thus, analogously, God's goal in creating the world was
the creation of man.   From among the races, the children
of Israel were selected to receive His Law and commandments, through the fulfillment of which they could merit
eternal life.   In order that the children of Israel might
earn their reward by fulfilling the law and the commandments, God created in them an evil *yezer* (inclination)
as an obstacle to their execution of perfect deeds.   When
they triumph over this evil *yezer* they are rewarded.   But
if, on the contrary, they do not subdue the evil *yezer*
they are punished.   If there were no evil *yezer* in the
world, and the Hebrews were innately either wholly
righteous or wholly wicked, they would deserve neither
reward not punishment.

Since the creation of an evil *yezer* was necessary for the
spiritual development of the children of Israel it was
essential to create the body of the crudest possible corporeal substance, so that the evil *yezer* would have the
power to dominate.   Were man to be created of fine,
spiritual substance, then the evil spirit could not have
this sway.   Consequently, the creation of an evil spirit
would be in vain.

To fashion such a creation, and to make room for manifested worlds in which neither beings could abide, the Supreme Emanator, the Infinite, the Origin of all Roots and the Cause of all Causes, willed to contract His Infinite Light, which extended through out all Being.

If not for the contraction, the owerwhelming abundance of Light would cause the disappearance of all the worlds, for existence is nothing but a succession of condensations of Light essence. Were this Light to shine alike everywhere, then all the worlds would be similar and totally invisible.

In order to reduce the too powerful downpour of His Light upon the nether beings, God established "Coverings" to sheild them. These coverings consist of an arrangement of planes which restrain the Light and cause its successive minimization and densification. Thus the Light is steadily decreased and densified, in a succession of condensations; and it is from the densest possible stage of Light that the body of man is created.*

Beware of thinking even for a moment that there is any change within the Creator Himself. Such an idea is unthinkable, for changes pertain only to the recipients of Light, according to their distance or proximity to the Source, the Creator. Think, for example, of a lighted candle that is placed before a person. If many veils were interposed, so that the person could enjoy but very little of the candle light, this would not mean that a change

---

* Translator's note. As the Light is extended from the Source into the worlds, it becomes progressively dimmer, according to its degree of remoteness from the source.

took place in the light itself, but rather in the person, who could not see the candle light because of the intervening veils.

The identical situation obtains in creation. There is no change in the Creator, but only in the recipients. Similarly, the ten *Sefirot* (Emanations) act as "veils"— ten stages, vessels or degrees which the Creator issued to serve as channels through which His bounty might be transmitted to man: restraining that bounty to the extent that the worlds shall not disappear because of the too great abundance of Light, yet providing a sufficient amount of it to ensure their continued existence. He therefore made ten vessels in order that the bounty, in traversing them, would become so densified that the lower creations could bear it. These ten vessels, or *SEFIROT* are as follows:

1.
KETER
(CROWN)

3		2
BINAH		HOKMAH
(INTELLIGENCE)		(WISDOM)

5		4
GEBURAH	DA'AT *	HESED
(POWER)	(KNOWLEDGE)	(MERCY)

6
TIF'ERET
(BEAUTY)

---

* TR. N. *KETER* and *DA'AT* are interchangeable terms.

7
HOD
(GLORY)

8
NEZAH
(TRIUMPH)

9
YESOD
(FOUNDATION)

10
MALKUT
(KINGDOM)

These *Sefirot* represent supervision of the worlds in terms of charactristics like: Mercy, Judgment, Compassion, Etc.; these characteristics are embodied in three pillars, with the right column, consisting of the *SEFIROT* Hokmah (Wisdom), Hesed (Mercy) and Nezah, (Triumph) representing Mercy and the left column, consisting of Binah (Intelligence), Geburah (Power) and Hod (Glory) representing the pillar of Judgment, while the central column, consisting of *Da'at* (knowledge) *Tif'eret* (Beauty) and *Yesod* (Foundation), is the pillar of Compassion. There is not a Light emitted by the Emanator, which is not inclusive of Mercy, Judgment and Compassion. These Lights issue neither separately, nor individually; instead, they emerge from the three pillars already intermingled. It is this fusion of the principles of Judgment, Mercy, and Compassion that supervises the governing of the world.

These ten *Sefirot* are named in accordance with the image of man. Thus, *Keter* is the cranium of the head; *Hokmah* and *Binah* are the two lobes of the brain within the head; *Hesed* and *Geburah* are the two hands (or the two sides); *Tif'eret* and the remaining *Sefirot* are the body.

Each of these *Sefirot* is constructed of ten Lights, each of which in turn is composed of an equal number of Lights and so on *ad infinitum*. When, in one of these vessels only a single light is illuminated it is called a *Sefira*. When all ten Lights in a vessel is illumined then it is defined as a *Parezuf* (Person). In order that it may be called a complete and perfect *Parezuf*, every division within must shine with all its Light so that the number of Lights will total six hundred and thirteen—the number of parts in a man's body.* Only then is it considered complete.

There are but five *Parezufim* (Persons) in all, for not every *Sefira* of the ten had the power to radiate in the manner just described. Only *Keter, Hokmah, Binah* and *Malkut* could do so. They are called respectively; 'ARIK ANPIN (Macroprosopus)—(*Keter*); ABA and IMA (Father and Mother) (*Hohmah* and *Binah*) and NUKBA (the Feminine Polarity) (*Malkut*). But the six remaining Sefirot, *Hesed, Geburah, Tif'eret, Nezah, Hod* and *Yesod*, did not have the individual power to radiate as forcefully as the others. Collectively, however, these lost six *Sefirot* build up a *Parezuf;* it is called ZEIR ANPIN (Microprosopus) — Tif'eret).

The ten *Sefirot* are united with the Creator Himself, just as the flame is annexed to the live coal. Although manifold hues are visible in the flame, close examination

---

* 613 also equals the required number of good deeds in a man's life.

reveals that there is but one flame attached to the coal. So it is with the *Sefirot*, they are irrevocably bound to the Creator and cannot be severed from Him. He is enclothed in them, as in garments. But, unlike a man's clothing, these "garments" are not removable. Rather, they resemble the outer skin of a caterpillar, which is an integral part of its body. The Emanator perpetually animates the *Sefirot*. Otherwise they could not exist. Bear in mind that the Emanator issued all these diversified degrees of Light for the purpose of maintaining the world. At times the world must be governed by Mercy, at other times it requires Judgment, or Compassion.

Although the bounty that flows from the Emanator into the *Sefirot* is of uniform quality, it changes within the individual degree in accordance with its nature. For example, two persons, one of a robuts noture and one of a more delicate nature, partake of a similar meal. Although they both consume the same food and are both sustained thereby, their levels of energy will differ. The same principle applies to the different pillars of the heavenly government. God's bounty strengthens the *Sefirot* so that they are enabled to function according to their diversified natures; therefore, the differences lie within the *Sefirot* themselves and not in the bounty.

Some of the *Sefirot* are perfect in themselves. These serve the purpose of maintaining the world. There are the others which are imperfect and can only be perfected through the actions and service of man. These imperfections have been pre-arranged for the benefit of man: should he help perfect the weaker *Sefirot*, he will be rewarded; should he incur further defects in them, he will be punished.

Defect inplies that the *Sitra Ahara*, or evil spirit, lays hold of a particular *Sefira* and interferes with its ascent to the Origin, where it could receive its share of bounty in order to transmit it to those below it. For that reason the evil spirit is characterized as bearing the weight of a stone, for when it seizes the *Sefirot*, it adds weight to them so that they cannot rise. The Emanator willed the existence of the evil spirit in the world as an instrument for the punishment of the wicked.

The extended Lights are symbolized by the letters of the Hebrew alphabet. Combinations of letters connote the brightness of upper Lights upon which the degrees are built. Because all the outlines of the letters are the result of ink strokes directed either to the right, to the left, or to the center, they symbolize Lights that are directed either to the right, to the left or, to the center. And just as the letters are black against the white paper, so are the degrees "black fire" against "White fire."

When we say that the Creator contracted His Light in order to make room for the worlds, this does not mean that He entirely withdrew His Light and failed to shine into the worlds—it is even impossible to entertain such an idea. For if such were the case, then the worlds could not exist even for one second. What it does mean is that from that place where He desired to extend *Sefirot,* He concealed His Light, veiling it so that it should not illumine with the same degree of power as previously. This was done so that the extension of the lower realms could become manifest, for otherwise they would be submerged in the Light and would remain dormant. Of what avail is a candle in the powerful light of midday sun? And this is precisely what is meant by "black fire against white fire". Wherever there is an extension of the Light for a nether being, that Light is named "black fire"; and wherever the Light of the Emanator is revealed, it is called "white fire". The Light of the nether being is a garment to the upper Light, for it "enclothes" the latter.

Bear in mind that the whiteness of the paper can be seen even in the very midst of the characters or letters. Similarly with the *Sefirot;* when the extension of a lower degree is completed, the upper Light immediately shines into it, and although it is not apparent, it is assuredly there. The Light is invisible because of the barrier which exists in the lower degree. For example, a candle light that is screened by shades will not shine through at a point where the shades are placed. Yet we who are seeing only the shades, cannot claim that there is no candle shedding its light behind them. Remove the obstructing shades, and we see the candlelight. It is the same with the Infinite Light, which appears in all the degrees. It is invisible because the nether being covers it. The Creator desired that the Light be veiled in order to grant existence to the lower beings, which could not otherwise survive in its full presence.

This is what the sages refer to when they say that by means of the twenty-two letters the world was created; that all the *Sefirot* came into existence through the combinations of the letters. All levels of being were created by means of the four-lettered Holy Name; YUD'HE WAW HE', or Tetragrammaton. As there are four letters in the Holy Name "Havaya" where the upper point of the Yud is concealed, so in the *Sefirot* there exist four worlds which are revealed, while a fifth one is concealed, and is not included in the number of the degrees. These are the four worlds of *Azilut*, (Emanation), *Beriah* (Creation), *Yezirah* (Formtion) and *Asiah* (Action). The *En Sof* (Infinite World) is that which is concealed.

The *Parezufim* (*Persons*) are likewise four in number: *Aba* and *Ima, Zeir Anpin* and *Nukba*. There is also a fifth, the *Parezuf* of *'Arik Anpin*, which is concealed.

Each entity, each world, is divided into five *Parezufim*, and each *Parezuf* comprises ten *Sefirot*. In order to link the worlds together, the Emanator caused the *Sefira Malkut* of the upper world to be clothed within the entire next lower world. One *Sefira* is capable of pervading an entire world, for each *Sefira* from a preceding world is equal to the whole of the succeeding world. Thus, *Malkut* of each world enclothes the world which succeeds it. The order is as follows: *Malkut* of Adam Kadmon or Primordial Man, which is *Malkut* of *En Sof*, is enclothed in *Azilut; Malkut* of *Azilut* is enclothed in *Beriah; Malkut* of *Beriah* is enclothed in *Yezirah; and Malkut* of *Yezirah* is enclothed in *Asiah*. The manner in which they penetrate each succeeding world, will be explained later. All the worlds are bound together by a powerful tie, the lower with the upper and the upper, in turn, with that which is above it, until we reach back to the bond with the Creator, whereby they are joined to Him in indissoluable unity.

Do not err, in reading the expressions "person" (*parezuf*), "vessel", or similar words denoting material forms, by concluding that such shapes or images actually exist in the upper realms. It is forbidden to even express such ideas, as it is stated in the Bible: "For ye saw no manner of similitude . . ." (Deuteronomy IV, 15). The Emanator, blessed be He, sends forth His Light in order to grant existence to the lower worlds. But of the precise manner in which this process takes place, no one may know. Only the Emanator bears this knowledge within Himself. The *Sefirot* are nothing but the very Light of the Emanator Himself. It is the identical Light sent forth without limit or barrier, or space restriction. However, the presence of diversity, when the Light is arranged in degrees, signifies that the extended Lights contain a greater proportion either of Mercy or of Judgment. The Creator stipulated these proportions to fit the needs of the world which He desires to sustain.

Each *Sefira* has a specific function in the administration of the world, and therefore must be illumined in accordance with its type of supervision. The same principle applies to the extension of the *Parezufim*. They are Lights which, when extended below, differ in their composition because the Creator is aware that a stipulated number and quality of degree is necessary for the governing of the world. The extension of the degrees therefore took place in the following manner: When there arose in the Creator's most pure and simple will the desire to manifest creation (which was to receive His

Light in measured and limited proportion) He Emanated His Light in a successive pattern of descending degrees until the present creation came into being. He did this, providing the finite and measured bounty necessary for the existence of the worlds, by "making room" for them, so to speak; by both concealing His infinite, immeasurable Light and concurrently extending it and sending it forth. By this process of extension, which signifies delimitation, the *Sefirot* came into being. This procedure continued until the density of Light reached the stage where it could be received by the worlds. This entire process of the extension of Light in descending degrees was aimed at the revelation of the created worlds. If not for the extension of the degrees, nothing material could have existed.

In fact the entire extension of being is more than the varying combinations of Lights which issue downward and become, by successive degrees, so dense and obscure as to permit the manifestation and continued existence of creation. Had there been no creation, there would have been no veil, no obstruction whatsoever to the mighty power of the Light, since in the absence of all created being, there would be no danger of anyone not being able to receive it. This is what is meant by the statement made at the outset that "what comes to the mind first is brought into action last". Thus, the Creator's initial Thought was to create man, but man had to come at the end of all His deeds. Before creating man, God was obliged to prepare the Lights in such a way that when a man appeared on the scene, he would find the bounty and sustenance necessary for his existence. Were man to come into being at the very outset only to find the Light stretched out infinitely without measure or limit, his creation would be pointless, for he would instantly disappear. Man's body is built of dense material substance (clay) and it can only bear Light which is modified to conform to its nature.

We must bear in mind that anything that seems materialistic or corporeal regarding the extension of creation must not be taken in a literal sense. This materialistic language ought not to be employed at all in a discussion of spiritual qualities; nevertheless we must assign them corporeal names in order to exemplify them, and thus facilitate understanding of this knowledge by man. These terms must be understood in their true sense, and everything is to be understood as a spiritual extension from the Infinite, Who spreads His Light in order to give existence to the nether beings and to govern them. The measure of Light which He sends forth to maintain and supervise is in accordance with what He wills to exist below.

The *Sefirot* are but the Will of the Creator Who willed their presence below. Thus they are actual and not merely potential forces. The names we attach to them are only figurative. They are symbolic names and are employed with reference to the recipients upon whom the bestowal is made. For example, by the term "vessel" we mean radiating Light, which, when extended down below, becomes a vessel. It is the same with a Light termed "Person" (*Parezuf*), which, as we already know, is a rediation of Light spread into 613 Lights.

Hence, all the *Sefirot* are nothing but the Light of the Infinite Himself. There is no difference between Him and the *Sefirot*—only He is the Cause and they are the effect, or the result. The expression "He clothes them" means that His will perpetually animates the *Sefirot* in order to maintain them as channels, through which He controls and governs the world.

Chapter Two

The Creator's chief aim is to bestow Goodness upon the created beings, and it was to this end that he wrought the varying stages of Light in accordance with the limited capacity of the nether beings. What follows is the ordered sequence of the individual stages, and the manner in which they issued forth.

The first *Parezuf* which was manifested in the worlds was Adam Kadmon, (the Primordial Man); all the subsequent stages and the *Parezufim* resulted from him. He is united with the Emanator Himself and is very much concealed. We cannot say anything whatsoever about the Primordial Man, but can treat only of the branches that ramify from him to the outside.

From this Primordial Man come many worlds— worlds without number. Of them all, we shall discuss the four worlds called "Seeing," "Hearing," "Smell" and "Speech," otherwise known as "Wisdom," Intelligence," "Beauty" and "Kingdom". They issue from the *eyes,* from the *ears,* from the *nose* and from the *mouth* of Adam Kadmon. Let us deal first with the world of Hearing, since it was the first of the four to be revealed.

As we stated in the introductory chapter, all created beings and *Parezufim* are divided into four categories, corresponding to the four letters in the Holy *"Havaya,"* and all of them originate in this Name. The Primordial

Man also has in Himself one four-lettered *Havaya* from the four letters of which four fully spelled-out *Havayas* issue, amounting respectively to 72, 63, 45 and 52.* These Names represent the *Ta'amim, Nekudot, Tagim* and *Otiot.***   Each one of these comprises all the other

---

* Tr. Notes 1. The Name which issues from the first letter "Yud", spelled:

(10) Yud	(6) Waw	(4) Dalet
(5) He'	(10) Yud	
(6) Waw	(10) Yud	(6) Waw
(5) He'	(10) Yud	

Having a numerical value of 72;

2. The Name originating in the first "He'" spelled the same as the first with the exception of the Waw which is spelled (6) Waw (1) Alef (6) Waw, and amounting 63;

3. The Name originating in the letter "Waw", spelled out with Alef's, thus:

(10) Yud	(6) Waw	(4) Dalet
(5) He'	(1) Alef	
(6) Waw	(1) Alef	(6) Waw
(5) He'	(1) Alef	

amounting to 45;

4. The Name which spring from the last "He'", spelled:

(10) Yud	(6) Waw	(4) Dalet
(5) He'	(5) He'	
(6) Waw	(6) Waw	
(5) He'	(5) He'	

amounting to 52.

** *Ta'amim* are the signs indicating pitches to be used in reading the Torah; *Nekudot* are the vowels sounds; *Tagin* are the ornamental strokes above certain letters; and the *Otiot* are the letters of the alphabet themselves.

four.*** Of the first stage, that is, of *Ta'amim* of the first Name, "72", we cannot speak, because It is in the Cranium of the Primordial Man and that is a deeply concealed place.

We shall now begin from the ears, which are the starting point of the extension of *Ta'amim* of the Name 63. As asserted above, every Name comprises all the four: *Ta'amim, Nekudot, Tagin* and *Otiot.* Now, just as there are three kinds of *Ta'amim* those placed above the letters, e.g. "Zareka", (∼) "*Pazer*" (μ) etc.; those placed beneath the letters, e.g. Darega, (s) T*evir*, (.,) etc.; and those placed in the middle of the letters, e.g. *Pesik*, (:) and *Makaf*, (—) there are likewise three kinds of Lights, one greater than the other, emanating from these *Ta'amim*, which are situated in the three places: ears, nose and mouth. See how the numerical value of the Name 63 is intimated in each place of emanation. Thus, the word *Ozen* (Ear) together with *He'*, the second letter of the *Havaya,* which is its Origin, amounts to 63. The He' (value of which is five numerically) points to the fact that from it five *Parezufim* are sent forth.

The word *Hotem* ("Nose") also points to the Name 63, as its numerical value is 63.

The word *Peh* (Mouth), which has a numerical value of 85, embraces this Name plus the 22 letters which are comprised in the five articulations of speech, since these have their source in the mouth. The five possible

---

*** The *Ta'amim* for example comprise in themselves the *Nekudot, Tagin,* and Letters, and it is the same with the others.

articulations of the mouth are: A-H-H', G-I-K-K, Z-S-SH-R-Z, D-T-L-N-T, B-W-M-F.

From the ears, then, came forth the upper *Ta'amim*. They extended from them as ten interior *Sefirot* and ten encircling *Sefirot*. From the right ear came the encircling, and from the left, the interior *Sefirot*. These two qualities are refered to as ten complete *Sefirot*. The *Sefirot* that were issued bound themselves together in absolute unity, so much so, that only a He' was apparent giving a hint of five *Parezufim*.

The graphical description of the *He'* is a *Dalet* together with a *Waw*, to designate that the emanation is really ten. But they are united so closely that nothing but a *He'* is discernible. The reason why the interior light issued at a distance from the *encircling Light* is that had these Lights been intermingled, it would have been necessary to produce a vessel in order to limit the immensity of the Light, as in the case of the Mouth below, wherethere is a vessel. Since, because of the tenuous light, it was impossible for a vessel to be revealed here, the Lights had to go forth at a considerable distance from each other. This division serves the same purpose as would a vessel, for it reduces the light. These Lights encircle, and hover over the Face extending down to the center of the Beard. The *encircling Lights* issue from the right Ear and the inner Lights issue from the left, because the encircling Lights are more tenuous than the inner ones. Thus, the *encircling Light* was left to encircle or hover over the vessel, because, due to its tenuity it could not be confined in the interior of the vessel.

The *inner Light*, which is not so tenuous, is confined in a vessel.

From the right side, which is always more tenuous than the left (since it represents the source of Mercy) there came forth the more tenuous, encircling Light. And from the left side, which is not so tenuous, because it represents the source of Power, there issued forth the inner, more definite Light.

We shall now discuss the world of "Smell," which is the second world to be revealed, and which issued from the Nose of Adam Kadmon. These are the middle *Ta'amim*. They issued in the same manner as those that came from the ears, that is, as ten inner and ten *encircling Lights*. From the right opening of the nose issued the *encircling Lights*, and from the left opening issued the inner Lights. Here the Lights were closer to each other than those of the Ears. We have concrete proof of this when we observe the nose of man, wherein the nostrils are closer to each other than are the ears. Nevertheless, we still have two separate passages capable of absorbing the diminished Light and thereby eliminating the revelation of vessels in this case as well as in the case of the ears.

But because the two Lights of the Nose are closer together than those of the Ears, something different was revealed here which was not revealed with the outflow of the Ear, namely, the *Vav* of the *He'*. In the Lights of the Ears the single He' alone was seen, and the *Waw* was concealed. But here in the nose the constituent parts of the *He'*—the *Dalet Waw*—were revealed.

The truth hinted at by the revealed *Waw* is that the Nose represents Beauty, which is *Z'O* or *Zeir Anpin*, or Microprosopus and comprises six *Sefirot*.

These Lights spread out over the Face just as did those of the Ears, hovering over the Face and reaching as far as the Chest.

The world of Speech, issuing from the mouth of Adam Kadmon, was the third to be revealed. These Lights are the lower *Ta'amim*. They, issued forth in the same manner as the others, namely as ten inner and ten *encircling Lights*. The difference is, however, that all these Lights merge and emanate through a single channel. Because of this, a type of vessel which reduces the Light originates here. Still it is but one single vessel, and furthermore, it is exceedingly tenuous because of the supreme exaltation of this realm. For it is in the mouth that is revealed what in the ears and the nose remained concealed. In the ears, a *He'* only was disclosed, and the nose, the *Waw* of the *He'* was manifested but here in the mouth, the *Dalet* of the *He'* is also *unveiled.**
The secret of this unveiled *Dalet*, which is equal to the number 4, is as follows: In the ears and nose there were only two types—the inner and encircling, but in the mouth, there are four types, since it is here that a vessel originated. Hence, two additional types of Lights were re-

---

* The *He'* alone represents but five collective *Parezufim*, which are also the ten *Sefirot* indicated by the *Dalet* (4) and *Waw* (6) that make up *He'*; but the hidden representations symbolized by this *Dalet* and *Waw* are only shown later as they are revealed through the nose and mouth.

vealed in the mouth, and those are the interior and the exterior of the vessel. Thse Lights issue from the mouth of Adam Kadmon, and reach to his navel.

Three distinct Lights, corresponding to the three different *Ta'amim*, issued from Adam Kadmon. These Lights issued from the ears, nose and mouth, and reached, respectively, the middle point of the beard, the chest, and the navel.

Remember that the names and characteristics which we employ here: "ears", "nose", "mouth", pertain only to the latter worlds, starting from the world of Emanation down, because it is there that a *Parezuf* (person) is revealed. In the exalted realm which we are now discussing, there is no evidence of a *Parezuf*. Nevertheless, in order to clarify the subject in question we must employ such anthropomorphic terms.

To turn back to the world of "Speech", otherwise known as the Bound World, or *Olam Ho-akudim*; these are the ten *Sefirot* which issued from the mouth of Adam Kadmon and reach to his navel. Because this was the first place where a vessel was revealed, only a single long vessel consisting of ten lights was discerned.

Note that these *Sefirot*, which issued in the mouth, were distinguished by the quality of *Nefesh* (Animal Soul) *alone*. They were not able to remain in the vessel and were obliged to return to their source to be emended. The vessel was wrought through the departure of the Lights. Later, the Lights returned and spread below once more.

Because all ten Lights were bound together in one vessel, they are designated as "Bound" (*Akudim*). This is derived from Biblical expression *"akudim"* used when Abraham *bound* Isaac in order to bring him as an offering to God. ". . . and bound Isaac his son." (*Genesis XXII, 9*).

In order that the vessel might not be annulled by too great an abundance of Light, when the Lights returned they did not descend to their original place, for the Light of the Crown remained concealed in its source and was not extended below. The Light of "Wisdom" (*Chokmah*) issued, occupying the place of Crown, and the succeeding Lights entered consecutively the vessels following "Crown". In this way "Kingdom" (*Malkut*) was left without Light. This is why Kingdom is considered a "non-luminous Mirror".

The departure of Lights, as described above, is designated as a minor annulment, but not an *actual* annulment such as occurred in the world of *Nekudim*, which will be dealt with later.

Chapter
Three

We shall now discuss the world of Points or *"Neku-dim"*, which is the world of "Seeing" or "Vision". Last revealed world of those four mentioned earlier, it issued from the eyes of Adam Kadmon. Because all the other apertures are filled with the Lights of *Ta'amim* of the Name 63, the Lights of *Nekudim* found no passage, except through the Eyes. They are the *Nekudot* of the Name 63.

What procedure did Adam Kadmon follow in order to issue these? He contracted his Light, which was spread below in His body, bringing it up above the Navel. Then he placed a veil over the middle of the body to restrain the Light from descending. The idea of his contraction is similar to what we say regarding ZO'N, or Microprosopus and his Feminine Polarity, of the Emanated World, when they rise as M'N (Returning Light) to the Father and Mother of the Emanated World. The same thing takes place here: that is, the Names of Adam Kadmon amounting to 45 and 52 respectively (these being his Microprosopus and Feminine Counterpart) rose as M'N to his Name 6 x 3 in order that 63 and 72 might unite and through the union bring forth these Lights.

The reason this union was required in bringing forth these Lights, though it was not needed for the Lights of the ears, nose or mouth, is as follows: the eyes, through which these Lights had to pass, were illuminated by the very powerful Lights of the Name 72, which resides in the brain and this Light veiled these Lights of *Nekudot* so that they could not pass through. Therefore the union took place, causing this Light of the Name 72 to be hidden within the Name of 63, that is, in the *Sefira* of Yesod (Foundation) of the *Parezuf* Mother. Thus, the Light (of 72) shone to a lesser extent than previously, lending the Lights of *Nekudot* sufficient Power to pass through.

Although these Lights issue from the eyes, they become visible only at the point below the navel. The reason for this is that the Lights of *Ta'amim* are spread throughout the region extending to the navel. Therefore the Lights of *Nekudot* are invisible only down to the end of the extension of *Ta'amim*.

These Lights which issued from the eyes were solely comprised of *Nefesh*, or animal soul. Therefore they are called "Kings" because they originate from the Name 52 which equals the numerical value of the letters spelling *Malkut*, "Kingdom". Because much *Din* (Justice) was intermingled with these lights, the husk or shell of power was engulfed therein. For the essence of the husk is none other than the might of rigid Justice, which is so exceedingly obscure, that it completely hinders the Light. The husks can only exist in the presence of much Justice.

Subsequently when the Light of Adam Kadmon, which is absolute purity, descended to be spread into the *Nekudim*, they could not bear it and so they broke.*

The circumstances behind the shattering of the vessels are as follows.

We have already stated previously that all the stages of extended Light are also represented by combination of letters. These are the functioning Lights from which everything comes into being. Since they were unable to endure the abundance of Light, the combination of letters became disarranged and were severed from each other. They were thus rendered powerless to act and to govern. This is what is meant by their "shattering". From that point on their husks, or shells, still engulfed by the Light, became energized. This energy was invigorated even further when the husks descended below into the material realm. The Supreme Emanator willed the "shattering" in order to sever the husk from the Divine Spirit so that It would remain without dross; in addition, He willed the existence of this obstruction to the Light, the husk, as a vehicle for the execution of

---

*Tr. N. By "breakage" we mean a change of phase or appearance. In this case, that the Nekudim lost their original governing powers and that a different aspect of supervision was assigned to them; for out of these Lights many combinations were wrought. Thus, that which, to begin with, was Emanation, became—following the shattering of the vessels—Creation, Formation and Action. This was their debasement at the time of the shattering of the vessels. But later, at the time of emendation, they were combined in a different manner so that they became the four worlds of *Azilut, Beriah, Yetzirah,* and *Asiah* (A'B'Y'A.)

reward or punishment. Consequently, when man sins, he gives the husk the power to seize the Upper Degrees, and hs is himself punished by it. Conversely, when man expels the husk from himself, he is rewarded. The following will illustrate the matter more fully.

The main shattering occurred in the seven lower *Sefirot**—in Z'O (Microprosopus and his Feminine Polarity) of the world of Emanation, to whom death is attributed. The front and hind *Sefirot* of these seven lower degrees were lowered still further, and descended into the worlds of Creation, Formation and Action (B'Y'A.).

In this fashion, the innermost part of each vessel descended into Creation; the interior part (which was next to the innermost) descended into Formation; and the exterior part descended into Action. The effect on the first three *Sefirot* (Crown, Wisdom, and Intelligence) was only that of annulment, rather than debasement. Only the rear portion of the first three *Sefirot* "fell"; and even this rear portion did not descend any lower than the world of Emanation, as did the seven lower *Sefirot*. It is for this reason that no "death" is attributed to the first three.

When Crown, Wisdom, and Intelligence were issued, they were placed in the order of pillars, that is, right, left and center, the essential order for emendation. All the *Sefirot* must eventually attain this order of three pillars; nevertheless, only the first three were sufficiently

---

* These are: Mercy, Power, Beauty, Triumph, Glory, Foundation and Kingdom.

organized to bear the Light that came from Adam
Kadmon and were therefore not shattered. On the
other hand, the seven lower *Sefirot* had issued one below the other; they had no order or emendation whatsoever, but were all disunited. In this condition, unable
to bear the infinitely pure Light, they broke and descended
below.*

There is intimation of the shattering of these seven Kings
in the Bible, Genesis XXXVI, starting with verse 31.
Note that "death" is mentioned for every King but

---

* Bear in mind that the descent we speak of here does not
refer to motion from one place to another. We have already
specified that the *Sefirot* are spiritual extensions from the Infinite,
employed to create the world. He sends forth His light in order
to sustain them. To reiterate: it is improper to attribute to anything in the spiritual realm either image or place. Thus, by the
expression "debasement from the world of Emanation to the
stage of B'Y'A", we mean that when the Light of Adam Kadmon
descended to enter the vessels they could not receive it, that is,
they could not unit with it, and were shattered and descended
below. From their original degree which, before the shattering,
was called "Emanation", they descended to an inferior degree
called B'Y'A. (One must remember that whenever the words
"ascent" or "descent" are mentioned in connection with Lights,
they refer to changes in their governing power, to either greater or lesser degree, in accord with the need of the moment, or the merit of the lower beings.) From these vessels,
various parts were selected. Only the most exalted and ample
portions of the vessels themselves—those which were far removed
from the root of the impure spirit (shell)—rose to unite with the
Light. The remainder of the vessels became B'Y'A', the worlds of
Creation, Formation and Action.

the eighth, the King of Hadar, for it was he who emended all the worlds.

The first king, *Bela*, stands for Knowledge (DA'-AT); he is a Light without a vessel, and does not therefore belong to the seven vessels or kings. Nonetheless, because he flows into them and forms their soul, he too is connected with "death".

The second, *Jobab*, son of *Zerah*, stands for Mercy (*Hesed*). The third, *Husham*, is Power (*Geburah*). The fourth, *Hadad*, is Beauty (*Tiphereth*). The fifth, *Samlab*, is Triumph and Glory (*Nezah* and *Hod*)— the two are considered as one because they are as the two halves (or thighs) of the body of Adam Kadmon. The sixth, *Saul*, is Foundation (*Yesod*). The seventh, *Baal-hanan*, stands for Kingdom (*Malkut*). But the eighth is King Hadar, and through him the emendation was effected. They are designated "Kings" because they originate in the Name 52, which, as we know, is the numerical value of the word "Kingdom".

The annulments occurring in the first three *Sefirot* were of varying degrees. Crown (*Keter*) was only annulled in the back portion of his Triumph (*Netzah*), Glory (*Hod*) and Foundation (*Yesod*). Actually, this is considered a defect, rather than an annulment. But in the remaining two *Sefirot* of the first triad— (*Hokmah* and *Binah'*) the entire rear sections were annulled. This happened because the Light of the ear, of which they partook, was of unequal power. Whereas Crown (*Keter*), which took the Light of the ear at a point where it shines most, was only partially affected. And this only happened because the last three *Sefirot*

of Crown—Triumph, Glory and Foundation—were enclothed in Father and Mother (Aba and Ima), the
inferior portion, and not because of Crown himself,
for he himself is complete and absolutely perfect.

Father and Mother (*Aba* and *Ima*), who partook
of the Light of the ear where it terminates, a point at
which it shines less powerfully, were therefore affected
by annulment throughout their hind part. But the
seven lower *Sefirot*, in whom the Light of the ears did
not shine at all, were unable to bear the powerful
Light and were therefore shattered. Although apparently
the shattering occurred only in the seven lower *Sefirot*
and not in the first three, this statement is only generally
true. For in the detailed portions of the *Sefirot* each
and every *Parezuf* was affected by all the consequences
connected with the "shattering": namely, the appearance of a defect in the rear part of Crown (comprised
of Truimph, Glory and Foundation); the annulment
of the rear parts of Father and Mother and the descent
of *their* seven lower *Sefirot*.*

---

* *Parezufim* are spoken of here although we are still at a
place in creation where there are no actual *Parezufim*. The
latter were only revealed following the emendation. The idea
is that the ten *Sefirot* of *Nekudot* comprised all that would later
come into being in all the *Parezufim* at the time of their manifestation as such. Thus, since these ten *Sefirot* broke, in the
order explained above, we find that all seven lower *Sefirot*, which
would later come into existence in all the *Parezufim*, are considered
to be shattered, too, and each "Wisdom" and "Intelligence" as
fallen, and every "Triumph", "Glory" and "Foundation" of every
"Crown" as being defective.

The whole incident of the shattering of the vessels is intimated in the verse of *Genesis* which says: "In the beginning God** created . . ." (Genesis I, 1). In other words, at the beginning God created the world with the measure of Justice, specifically, with those *Sefirot* embodying the quality of Justice. And then: ". . . the earth was empty and void." (Genesis I, 2) It could not bear the Light and was therefore annulled. Then the measure of Compassion, which is the "New Name Forty-five" was supplemented to Justice, and through It the emendation was effected. It was also through this Name that the worlds gained stability and permanence.

We shall now return to the subject of the shattering of the vessels and explain it in detail These vessels or newly-invented boundaries were not at first revealed, but only became apparent in the ten *Sefirot* of *Nekudot.* For as soon as the vessels had been invented, with its first contraction, the Light of the Emanator entered them in its full vigor and overpowered them, thereby preventing their manifestation and inhibiting their presence. But at the emanation of the ten *Sefirot* of *Nekudot,* the Light was diminished to such an extent that the vessels were able to triumph over It and become revealed.

Although, in speaking previously about the Lights of the Mouth of Adam Kadmon, that is, the Bound World, we said that a vessel was revealed, nevertheless

---

** Tr. N.   Here the Name for God, Elohim, indicating Justice, is used rather than *Havaya,* which stands for Mercy or Compassion.

it is not designated as a "revelation" for there was no
aggregation of vessels, but only a single vessel, which
might be referred to as a preparatory form of that which
was to be revealed in the world of *Nekudot.*   For the
entire Bound World, with all its contents, is nothing but
a preparatory state to the world of *Nekudot.*   Where
an actual revelation took place in that a vessel was revealed, together with all its contents, and was then
converted into ten vessels.   Because this revelation was
effected here, Justice grew so dense at this point that it
became the original root of the husk, or the *sitra ahara*
(evil).

For in truth the word "vessel" implies none other
than Justice (Din) which obstructs and completely shuts
out the Light. Therefore, at whatever place a boundary
begins to manifest, there the husk has a certain connection, for it obstructs and limits (the Light).

Because of the presence of the husks, the *Sefirot*
were not capable of complete emendation, for this would
mean that the husks would also be included in the three
parallel pillars of Mercy, Justice and Compassion, and,
as a result of their cohesive action, that they would op-
pose the work of the *Sefirot.* The Supreme Being had
no desire that the husks should issue from that which
was emended, but rather from that which remained unemended.   It was necessary then that the vessels descend
to that low point where the husks could manifest.

Subsequently, when the emendation took place, the
Sefirot were arranged in the form of pillars because the
root of impure powers had by then been expelled from

them. Note that while the vessels were themselves still
without Light, the root of the husk did not incur any
defect in them. The effect of the vessels' existence was
already so limiting that the presence of the root of the
husk became possible in them. But when the Light
approached to enter the vessels—and the quality of this
Light was such that the husk had no relationship whatsoever with it—it could not unite with the vessels.
Thus, in order to receive the Light that would permit
them to act and to govern cooperatively, the vessels were
obliged to descend so many degrees as were necessary to
cause the root of the husk to depart from them. For
as long as the root of the husk was within them, they
were unable to receive the Light. So they were shattered, and their form was changed.

Instead of remaining within the realm of Emanation, they became B'Y'A, the worlds of Creation, Formation and Action. Bear in mind that the degree of
Emanation prior to the shattering was superior to that
of the current Emanation, for its original power was
lost at the time of the shattering. But at the time of
emendation, four worlds were constructed out of the
three. Emanation is actually the inner essence of the
original world of Creation. Only the portions that belong to *Arik Anpin* (Macroprosopus)—Crown, Wisdom
and Intelligence—were left unaltered.

In the ten *Sefirot* of the *Nekudim* were comprised
all the *Sefirot* suitable for apportionment into all the
Parezufim. But their nature was such that in the event
of shattering, their form would change, and, following

emendation, they would be distinguished as the second
Emanation. However, to Arik Anpin alone was something supplemented. In addition to the ten *Sefirot* already belonging to it (as they did to all the other
Parezufim) Arik Anpin also had the Crown, Wisdom
and Intelligence of the original *Ta'amim* and *Nekudot*
which were neither changed nor weakened by the shattering. These three *Sefirot* rose to *Arik Anpin*; and by
virtue of this addition three Heads were fashioned:

1) *'Atik*—The Ancient
2) Kithra—Crown
3) *Hokmah Stimoe*—Concealed Wisdom

In taking this particular Crown at the time of
emendation, 'Atik assumed the Crown of the Name
forty-five. Likewise, *Arik Anpin* took *Hokmah* of the
Name "45" because it has *Hokmah* of the original
Emanation. Intelligence of the first Emanation, requiring "Father and Mother" (*Abba & Ima*),—for they are
but an extension of the brain—, took *Hokmah Stimoe*.
But the three Heads of *Arik Anpin* proper were constituted of Crown, Wisdom and Intelligence of the
second Emanation.

This is why we refer to two different triads of
Heads. In the first we count the Unknown Head as
one, and *Kithra* as two. In the second triad we do not
count the Unknown Head, but start from Kithra. There
are two kinds of Emanation. Thus, according to the
first Emanation the Unknown Head is the first Head,
Kithra is the second, *Hokmah Stimoe* is the third, because Crown, Wisdom and Intelligence are of this type;

but according to the second Emanation we do not count the Unknown Head because there is nothing in it of this type. *Kithra* is the first Head, since it is made of Crown of the second Emanation.

Similarly, at the time of emendation, all the rest of the *Parezufim* were made of the entities of the second Emanation, comprised in the *Sefirot* of *Nekudim*. Since they were issued only in the degree of the second Emanation, Father and Mother, "whose source is in "Wisdom" and "Intelligence" of *Arik Anpin,* instead of retaining their original place in its head, now enclothe only its arms.

Chapter
Four

We shall now outline the manner of the vessels' descent into the world of Creation, and their specific destinations therein.

To begin with, we must understand that the descent of the vessels and the descent of the Lights occurred simultaneously. However, the Lights remained in the world of Emanation proper, and did not descend below it. Their descent (even thus far) is not due to any defectiveness in the Lights themselves. For, as previously stated, defects are attributable only to vessels, since they represent a type of Justice and cannot bear the Lights, which represent Absolute Mercy.

The reason for the descent of the Lights in the world of Emanation resides in the fact that the vessels (also referred to as "Kings") were destined to rise to their places at the time of emendation. This could not take place if the vessels were so completely removed from the Light as to remain entirely obscured, unemended and therefore powerless to rise. To prevent this from taking place, the Emanator so arranged it that the individual Lights intended for each vessel shone into them from their places at a distance in such a manner that the darkness did not triumph over them.

We shall now explain the order of the descent of these Lights. When the Light of *Da'at* or Knowledge (the first of the seven Kings) came forth to reign and to shine in its place, its vessel was unable to bear it. Thus the vessel shattered and descended to the place where "Knowledge" in the world of Creation was eventually to abide. In order to shine into its vessel, the Light itself descended to the place of "Kingdom of Emanation," which is located in the world of Creation. The Light is located therefore at a distance of but three degrees from its vessel.

The arrangement is similar with each of the *Sefirot*, namely, the Light assigned to each vessel shines into it at a distance of three degrees. Note that the Light of "Knowledge", which went down to the vessel of "Kingdom," did not descend with its full might, for if it did, the vessel of Kingdom would break, thereby preventing the required flow of its Light from entering into the world of Creation. Only a small proportion of the Light—such as "Kingdom" could bear—entered to shine below through it into its already descended vessel.

Immediately after the descent of "Knowledge" the Light of "Mercy" was issued to reign and shine in its place. Thus *it* descended into *its* vessel. This vessel too could not bear the ample Light so that it too broke, and fell to the place of "Intelligence" in the world of Creation, while the Light descended to the place of "Foundation" in the world of Emanation, for the place of "Kingdom" was already taken by the Light of "Knowledge". There the Light of "Mercy" shone into its vessel also at a distance of three degrees.

Thereafter, "Power" was issued and its vessel, being unable to bear the might of its Light, shattered also. The vessel descended to the place of "Wisdom" of the world of Creation, and the Light occupied the place of "Triumph" and "Glory" in the world of Emanation. As was remarked, these two *Sefirot* are symbolic of the two halves of the body.

Then the Light of "Beauty" was issued and desired to reign in its place; its vessel broke and fell to the place of "Crown" of the world of Creation, but the Light remained in its place and shone from there into its vessel which was now located below. The Light of "Beauty" therefore differs from the other Lights, for they went below their places to shine into their vessels, while the Light of "Beauty" remained in its own place. From there it radiated forth to its vessel. Since it had not descended, the Light of "Beauty" retained its original strength. But the other Lights *had* descended, and although it was not due to any defect or lack in them, their power was thereby somewhat lessened from its original strength. Although these Lights remained without garments (vessels) to enclothe them, they had no desire to rise above from their places, since their original power no longer existed.

However, when the Light of "Beauty", standing in its full capacity of power, perceived that it had no garment (vessel), it desired to rise above to its place— namely the place of its issuance, which is "Intelligence." But this would entail complete separation between "Beauty" and its vessel, and the latter would remain unemended and entirely obscure. So the Supreme Emanator arranged that the vessel belonging to "Crown" (which had not been shattered) should extend and magnify its size until it reached below. This vessel is drawn by way of the middle pillar, for, as described above, the first three *Sefirot* were already arranged as pillars, even prior to the emendation. The vessel reached the place of "Beauty" and enclothed it halfway, to the place of the Navel. The other half, which remained bare, rose into the vessel of "Crown" and became concealed there.

Then the Light of "Knowledge", which had descended below to "Kingdom" of the world of Emanation, seeing a new vessel in its place (for "Knowledge" also has its place, in the central pillar, between "Crown" and "Beauty"), rose above to its place and its vessel descended to "Kingdom" of the world of Creation. Since its Light was remote from the vessel, the latter was unable to remain in its place, and so it descended below to "Kingdom".

But the vessel of "Beauty" did not descend, even with its Light far removed from it. For in the case of Beauty the distance is not designated as complete, since only half of the Light was concealed, and the other half remained in its place. Hence its vessel also did not move from the place to which it had descended— namely to "Crown" in the world of Creation.

With the ascent of the Light of Knowledge to its place, the vessel belonging to "Crown" was amplified at the position of "Beauty" and extended to the point where "Beauty" terminates. Then the lower half of "Beauty," the Light that had been concealed above, returned to its place; for the Light had originally ascended in response to the fact that "Crown's" vessel was reaching only halfway down along "Beauty". Perceiving its lack of enclothement, the lower half of the Light then rose above into the vessel. But now, the vessel of "Crown" was so full that it extended to the terminating point of the lower half of "Beauty" causing the Light to descend and return to its original place.

It is important to know how the upward ascent of "Knowledge" caused the magnification of the vessel of "Crown." There are two reasons: first, while the Light belonging to "Knowledge" passed through that vessel in order to ascend "Knowledge" enclothed it and the Light radiated therein, thereby amplifying the vessel of Crown. Secondly, "Knowledge" is a collective source for all the six lower *Sefirot.** It is their soul. Therefore when it rose, it gave power to the vessel of "Crown," and magnified it in order to permit the Light of "Beauty" to descend to its original place. It was possible for the vessel of "Knowledge" to go down as far as "Kingdom" in Creation, because the separation between the Light and the vessel was no greater than three degrees. Although the Light itself benefitted and the vessel suffered a lack, the loss was not great since the immediate welfare of the Light comes first and because it is obliged to shine into the vessel anyway.

In the beginning, when there was no vessel at the place of "Knowledge", the Light of "Knowledge" desired to

---

* Tr. N. "Mercy", "Power", "Beauty", "Triumph", "Glory", "Foundation".

shine into its vessel, since by so doing the vessel would benefit, and the Light itself would suffer no loss. For even if the Light had risen back to its place, it would have had no benefit whatsoever, since there was no vessel. Therefore, since it descended to shine into its vessel, it did not rise again.

However, now that a vessel came into being at the original place of "Knowledge", "Knowledge" ascended to it, for by virtue of its ascent it gained an advantage and acquired greater Light than the measure it had had below.

As for the lack in the vessel, this also does not amount to anything, for when we say that it is necessary for the distance between Light and vessel to be less than that of three *Sefirot*, we refer to three *Sefirot* of the world of Emanation, whose measure is extensive. Therefore if the Light were to be at a distance of three *Sefirot* of Emanation from the vessel, the vessel would be designated as entirely remote from the Light. But in this case, although the vessel of "Knowledge" descended to "Kingdom" in the world of Creation, its descent is not considered great, for it resides at the head of the world of Creation, and even all ten *Sefirot* of this world taken together do not equal the size of even one of the *Sefirot* in the world of Emanation

Furthermore, you may ask: How can it be that the Light of Knowledge is entirely remote from its vessel at a distance of three degrees of Emanation? The answer is as follows. When we say that the distance of a Light from a vessel must be no greater than three degrees, this does not refer to the distance between a vessel and its own Light, as will be explained later. What it does mean is that in order that the vessels shall not be completely remote from the Lights, it is sufficient for them to be within the stipulated distance of any Lights, for it does not matter if these Lights come from *Sefirot* other than their own.

Such is the case here: although the Light of "Knowledge" was considerably removed from its vessel, it made no difference, since at the end of Emanation there were other Lights from which this vessel could receive illumination. Or it could even receive its own Light through the agency of those adjacent Lights. This principle applies in the case of all the *Sefirot*. For there is never an instance in which, between the Light and the vessel, there are three *Sefirot* of Emanation empty of Light.

Now to complete the description of the *Sefirot*, starting from "Beauty" and moving downward. When the Lights of "Triumph" and "Glory" came forth to reign, they should have reigned in their own places. But their places were not free. The Light of "Power" had descended there, as described above. Then "Intelligence" extended her vessel and was drawn through the left pillar to the place which was to be specified for "Power". For these lower *Sefirot* were not as yet arranged in the order of pilars. When the Light of "Power" saw a new vessel in its place, it rose up while its own vessel descended into "Foundation" of the world of Creation. Because the Light was now further removed from the vessel, the power of the vessel was diminished, and it descended below. Following this, since they had been evacuated, "Triumph" and "Glory" reigned momentarily in their proper places, and their vessels broke, descending to the place of "Triumph" and "Glory" of the world of Creation. The Lights themselves rose up as far as "Power". The reason for their joint ascent to that point is that since "Triumph" and "Glory" are the two halves of the body, it is impossible for one to rise without the other. Therefore, when "Glory" rose up as far as "Power" (because Glory is part of the same left pillar as Power), "Triumph" (although it belongs to the right pillar) rose there as well.

Thereafter, the Light of "Foundation" came forth, but it did not proceed to its own place, since the Light of "Mercy" was occupying it. This necessitated the extension of the vessel of "Wisdom" by way of the right pillar all the way to the place where Mercy would be established after the Emendation. Then the Light of "Mercy" rose there and became included in the vessel of "Wisdom". "Mercy's" vessel descended into "Beauty" of the world of Creation, since its Light was now at a remote distance from it. Then "Foundation" reigned in its own place. Its vessel shattered and descended into "Power" of the world of Creation. Its Light rose by way of the central pillar up to the place of "Knowledge" of the world of Emanation.

Following that the Light of "Kingdom" came forth. Its vessel was unable to bear this Light, and it broke. Thus the vessel descended to the place of "Mercy" of Creation, and the Light rose to "Knowledge" by way of the central pillar, just as the Light of "Foundation" had done.

That is why the vessel of "Beauty" is located at "Crown" in the world of Creation, and the vessel of "Kingdom" at "Mercy" in the world of Creation, and there is no instance in which the distance between one vessel and another is greater than three degrees. Also, in the world of Emanation there is no space which is void of Light extending more than three degrees.

So much for the matter of the shattering of the "Kings". Now let us examine why the Lights of "Foundation" and of "Kingdom" rose up to "Knowledge" —that is, higher than the Lights of "Beauty". It is important to remember that the *Sefira* of "Foundation" possesses a special capability which gives it preference over the other *Sefirot* in that it is able to rise all the way up to the place of "Knowledge". In the writings of Isaac Luria explaining the uniting process between *Zeir Anpin* (*microprosopus*) *and* "Leah" during the *Minha* prayers, and how this union can take place when the Feet of "Leah" reach only to the Chest of Z'O. The solution is derived from what we have said, namely that at the time of the *Minha* prayer, one-third of the *Sefira* of "Foundation" rises to the upper third of "Beauty" of Z'O, and there unites with "Leah".

This matter is also alluded to in the *Zohar*, where Joseph (Foundation) is spoken of as being above, and below. He has this virtue because upon Foundation depends the union, and through it passes the generative seed, which issues from Knowledge and proceeds to the feminine polarity. If he had not this power of rising all the way to "Knowledge" (the soul of the six *Sefirot*), where the five Mercies which constitute the generative seed reside, "Foundation" would be unable to draw this seed from "Knowledge" itself in order to bring it down to the feminine polarity.

Since it is customary for "Foundation" to make the ascent to "Knowledge", we can see why, during the shattering of the vessels, the Light of "Foundation" rose up to "Knowledge", even surpassing "Beauty". Furthermore, the ascent was made in order to bind together all the six *Sefirot* and to transmit the illumination of "Knowledge" to them for *Da'at*, or "Knowledge" is the very soul of the Sefirot.

Now let us examine the ascent of "Kingdom" to the place of Knowledge. The matter is as follows: at the outset, when the vessel of "Knowledge" broke and separated from its Light, the Light descended to "Kingdom" in the world of Emanation, and although later this Light rose from "Kingdom" to "Knowledge" it still left its impression there. It is the nature of divine Lights to leave their "impression" when they depart from any particular place which they have occupied. It was from this impression of the Light of "Knowledge" that the Light of "Kingdom" derived its power to rise up. Moreover, the ascent of "Kingdom" represents a great accomplishment in the process of Emendation.

It has already been explained how and why the Lights of both "Triumph" and "Glory" rose to the place of the *Sefira* "Power". Now, with the rising of "Kingdom", "Triumph" separated itself from "Glory" and went to the right pillar, for that is its place. Thus, the impression of the Light of Knowledge left with Kingdom actually makes it "Kingdom" of "Knowledge", which is composed of the substance of the Powers in the *Sefira* "Knowledge". When "Kingdom" rose, therefore, this impression of Light rose with it. The impression, which derives from the Powers and is the diadem of the feminine polarity, united with the Mercies which reside in Knowledge, and are called the diadem of the masculine polarity; as a result of this union, "Knowledge" shone into the six *Sefirot*. The impression shone into the left pillar and caused "Glory" to remain in her proper place. The diadem of the masculine polarity, that is, the Mercies, shone into the right pillar, causing "Triumph" to separate from "Glory" and cross over to its proper place on the right pillar.

In this way all the six *Sefirot* were emended by virtue of the ascent of Kingdom.

All the vessels which descended into the world of Creation at the time they became defective, were selected, and emended during which time they ascended to their places. But they were not selected completely. Each and every day they continue to be selected and emended by means of our prayers. The power of the husks, which came into being because of these vessels, gradually declines as these selections are withdrawn from them. When the process of selection will have been completed, that is, when they will have been completely selected, then the husk will be entirely annulled. This will occur at the time of the final emendation, when the shell will be exterminated, and the Divine Power alone will remain.

On that eventful occasion, the Prophet tells us: "He will destroy death forever; and the Lord God will wipe away tears from off all faces . . ." (*Isaiah XXV*).

And it is also said: "And the Lord shall be king over all the earth: in that day shall the Lord be One, and His Name One." (*Zachariah XIV, 9*)

Chapter
Five

What follows is a description of the fall of the posterior parts of *Aba* and *Ima* (Father and Mother). We have already mentioned above that the fall of these posterior parts is different from the shattering of the seven lower *Sefirot,* for they descended to the worlds of Creation, Formation and Action, while these, although they descended from their degree, remained in the world of Emanation itself. It must also be borne in mind that the fall of the posterior parts of Father and Mother was not due to any shortcomings of theirs—for the breaking of the vessel is a result of its merger with the root of the evil spirit, which rendered the vessels unable to receive the Light or to unite with it. The vessels were shattered in order to be purified.

However, in the three first *Sefirot,* there is no trace of the root of a shell, or evil spirit. The fact that the other seven *Sefirot* were unable to issue in the arrangement of three pillars is proof that the evil spirit was rooted in them. But, since the evil spirit already had no connection with them, the first three *Sefirot* were arranged in the order of pillars. Nevertheless, they too were affected in that they were drawn down in the form of the brain of Adam Kadmon into the seven lower *Sefirot.*

As far as they themselves are concerned, they were emended so that they could sustain their own existence, but their emendation was not as great as that of the seven lower *Sefirot*. Instead, while their anterior portions remained unaffected, their posterior parts descended from their degree.

What we mean by the terms "anterior" and "posterior" are, respectively, parts that shine and parts that do not shine. They are the source of the "front" and "back" in man. Thus, when we speak of a condition of "face to face" or "back to back" in relation to *Parezufim*, we refer to a change of administration: that is, when the posterior part of the *Parezuf* is dominating, the anterior part is concealed—or vice versa. These alternate administrations result from changing cycles, or from the actions of mankind.*

Although the *Sefirot* "Wisdom" and "Intelligence" are *Nekudot* (Points), nevertheless we find in them the ability to see each other "face to face". This effects in them what resembles the union that is required for the issuance of the seven lower *Sefirot* which are as offspring to them, for actually they are drawn from them. For these two *Sefirot* (even only as Points) also comprise the appropriate parts that are later to be allotted to Father and Mother (*Aba* and *Ima*), to Israel the Ancient and Understanding (Israel *Saba* and *Tebunah*), at the time that they are subdivided into these four *Parezufim*. (Thus, the *Sefirot* of *Nekudot* comprise all the qualities pertain-

---

* TR. N. In brief, when the posterior part rules, and the Light is hidden from the world, it means that the world is under rigid Judgment; but when we speak of the anterior part ruling, then it means that the Light of Mercy is shining, and that the world is being governed through Compassion.

ing to all the *Parezufim* of Emanation, which are disclosed at the time they are manifested.)

During the time that the "Kings" (vessels) existed, Father and Mother were in a condition of being "face to face". But with their fall, Father and Mother suffered a diminution of all degrees, culminating in the fall of their posterior parts. The order of this diminution is as follows:

When "Knowledge" fell, simultaneously the two pillars, that is, Mercy and Power of "Knowledge" in Father and Mother, descended into the body. This deprived Father and Mother of the privilege of facing, that is, observing, each other.* When "Mercy" fell, the posterior part of Father descended, causing him to turn his back to the face of Mother. Then, instead of being, as at first, "face to face", they were changed into a condition of "face to back." When the vessel of "Power" fell, the posterior part of Mother descended, causing her to turn her back to the back of Father, who had previously turned. Thus they came to the condition of "back to back". When a third part of the vessel of "Beauty" fell, then the posterior parts of the "Foundations" Father and Mother descended.

When the remainder of "Beauty" fell, "Mercy" and "Power" of "Knowledge" in Israel the Ancient and Understanding, descended into the body. When "Triumph" and "Glory" fell, then the posterior part of Israel the Ancient and Understanding descended. Thus they

---

* TR. N. Since "Knowledge", which is their mediator, is no longer present to unite them.

too assumed the position "back to back". When "Foundation" fell, then the posterior part of their "Foundations" descended. When "Kingdom" fell, then the posterior parts of the "Crowns" of Israel the Ancient and Understanding descended.

Thus the corruption of the posterior parts of the *Sefirot* "Triumph", "Glory" and "Foundation" belonging to "Crown", was completed. The cause for the defect in "Triumph", "Glory" and "Foundation" of "Crown" was that they had been drawn in the form of brain into Father and Mother, and not because of any fault of their own. The posterior part of Father and Mother descended to the encircling Light of "Mercy" and "Power" in the world of Emanation. The posterior part of Israel the Ancient and Understanding descended into the anterior and posterior parts of "Kingdom".

Now you can see that the whole incident of shattering is one process, affecting the seven lower vessels and the four posterior parts of Father and Mother, and Israel the Ancient and Understanding. From these the husk was built. So that in our daily prayers we express *"Pitum Haketoret . . ."* the mixture of perfumes which comprises eleven different ingredients of incense, in order to select these eleven distinct entities of divinity from the husk. Their selection is to continue until the advent of the Messiah, for only then will they be completely extracted from the shells.

Chapter
Six

We shall now explain the subject of the 288 Sparks (in Hebrew RESH, PEH, CHET) which are often mentioned in discussions of the shattering of the "Kings". We have already described above the shattering of the seven lower *Sefirot* of the *Nekudim*, for in them alone, and not in the three first *Sefirot*, did the shattering occur. Their debasement means their death.

It is necessary to bear in mind the principle that all things existing in the world exemplify that which occurred in those "Kings". The death of man in this world is analogous of the descent of those "Kings". Thus, for example, when a person dies, the soul and the body separate from each other. The soul rises above to its abode, while the body descends to the earth, wherein it is buried. In the descent of those "Kings", the Lights separated from the vessels as the soul of a man separates from his body. The soul of the vessel (in their case, the Lights), rose above to its place in the world of Emanation, while the vessels themselves (corresponding to the body of a man) descended below to the world of Creation. This was their "burial". The emendation of these vessels, and their ascent, when that ocurs, instructs us regarding the event of resurrection, when the dead will be made living. The very bodies that were buried will rise, just as the vessels were raised at the time of selection.

Note that just as when a person dies, some spirit is left in his body, designated by the *Zohar* as the "heat of the bones", so that it may be sustained until the time of its resurrection, likewise, when those "Kings" descended, a small amount of spiritual power was left in them in order to sustain them during the period of emendation of the world of Emanation. This power is referred to as the 288 Sparks, which remained in the vessels when they descended to the world of Creation. However, the principal Lights departed to go above into the world of Emanation, leaving only a small part in the vessels to animate them. 288 Lights remain—this being the sum total of the four quantities of 72 Sparks which descended from the four Names: 72, 63, 45, 52.

At the outset, it is necessary to know that the superior entities of the Lights rose upward, while the inferior ones remained in the world of Creation. Now to explain the different degrees of strength in the Lights and the measure of superiority of one Light over another.

It is already known that the Lights of the world of Emanation are comprised of all the variations on the four *Havayas,* which are as follows:

1) *Havaya* totalling 72;
2)   „   „   63;
3)   „   „   45;
4)   „   „   52:

The principal Lights are the four simple (that is, not spelled out) letters of the Name *HAVAYA* when they appear in the shapes of the four Hebrew Letters. Thre is also another form, that is, when the *HAVAYA* is considered in its numerical value, as when we say that the four simple letters of the *Havaya* amount to 26. These two distinctions exist also in the "posterior" spelling of the Name, as well as in the fully-spelled Name, and again in the completed spelling of the fully-spelled Name. The process of permutation goes on *ad infinitum*. It is self-evident that the shapes of the letters themselves are considered more as origin and source of Creation than for the numerical value they yield.

The following outline describes the stages of the *Havaya* whose numerical value is 72. From this, all the other *Havayas* will be understood:

The *first stage* is the shape of the four simple letters, thus:

Y'H'W'H.

The *second stage* is the progression of the shape of the four simple letters, thus: Y Y'H Y'H'W' Y'H'W'H. They are ten letters in all. This is the backward aspect of the Name HAVAYA.

The *third stage* is the total of the simple four letters of the Havaya, which is 26. Y-10; H-5; W-6; H-5

The *fourth stage* is the total of the progression of the four letters, which is 72. Y-10; YH-15; YHW-21; YHWH-26

The *fifth stage* consists of the ten spelled-out letters of *Havaya*, thus: Y'W'D H'Y W'Y'W H'Y.

The *sixth stage* is the fully spelled-out progression when it appears as follows: Y'W'D; Y'W'D, H'Y; Y'W'D, H'Y, W'Y'W; Y'W'D', H'Y, W'Y'W, H'Y.

The *seventh stage* is the number 72, which represents the total of the spelled-out *Havaya*.

The *eighth stage*, totalling 184, is the numerical value of the progression of the fully spelled-out Name.

$$Y = 10 \qquad W = 6 \qquad D = 4 \times 2 \qquad = 40$$
$$H = 5 \qquad Y = 10 = 15 + 20 + 15 +$$
$$W = 6 + Y = 10 + W = 6 = 22 + 20$$
$$+ 15 + 22 + 15 = 184$$

In this manner, the stages proceed *ad infinitum*. And it is the same with the other Names. We must know that each preceding stage is superior to the one that succeeds it; recall that the Sparks that were left in the vessel are of the most inferior quality. It must also be borne in mind that Sparks originally descended from each of the four *Havayas* in order to animate their vessels. The sparks of the *Havaya* 72 descended into the vessels that belongs to 72. And the same is true of the others; since the Sparks of one *Havaya* have no power to animate the vessel belonging to a different *Havaya*, it was therefore necessary that Sparks should descend from each individual name.

It is necessary to know further that the *Havaya* of 72 is superior in quality to all the other *Havayas*. The next in degree is the *Havaya* 63; next to it is the *Havaya* 45; and below it is the *Havaya* of 52. Because of these variations in degree the manner of their descent is dis-

similar. Thus, in the Name 72—highest in degree—the
shattering was not so thorough. Its descending Sparks
were few. From the Name 63 more Sparks fell than
from 72, but less than those from the Name 45. From
the Name 45, more Sparks fell than from 63, but less
than what fell from the name 52. From 52 more Sparks
fell than from àll the others, for the name 52 is the
lowest of all.

The first six stages of the highest *Havaya*, 72, ascended to the world of Emanation. The remaining
stages—from the seventh on—together with their vessels
—descended to the world of Creation. However, those
stages which follow the seventh are not considered separately, but are included in the seventh, which is the only
stage that is counted. It is the sum of the ten letters of
the fully spelled-out Name, which amounts to 72.

From the Lights of the Name 63, only the first four
degrees rose to the world of Emanation. The two other
superior degrees descended to the world of Creation. They
are the fifth degree: the shapes of the ten spelled-out
letters of the Name; and the sixth degree, their posterior
part. When we count the ten spelled-out letters simply
as ten letters and add their numercial value, which is 63,
the total is 73.

From the Name 45, which is "Beauty," only two
upper degrees rose to the world of Emanation, since this
Name is lower in degree than 63. The remaining degrees
descended below. The third degree, which is the numerical value of the four letters of the Name *Havaya* and

the seventh degree, which is the numerical value of the
ten spelled-out letters, totals 71 (26 + 45).

From the Name 52, only the uppermost degree consisting of the four simple letters of *Havaya,* that is, the
letters themselves, rose to the world of Emanation. The
reason for this is that the Name 52 is in "Kingdom",
and is the lowest. Here the extent of the shattering was
greatest of all. Therefore, with the sole exception of the
first degree, which rose to Emanation, all the remaining
Lights of "Kingdom" were unable to rise upward and so
they fell into the World of Creation. This is the key to
the knowledge that "Kingdom" is but one Point; for
only the one of its Points, the first degree, remained in
the world of Emanation, and the remainder descended
below.

Hence, the 72 Sparks which fell from the Name 52
are the sum of the progression of the ten backwards
letters of the simple *Havaya* that amount to 72. From
the Name 72 we stipulate descent of the seventh degree
only, and from the Name 63, the fifth and the seventh,
and from the Name 45 the third and the seventh and
from the Name 52 only the fourth. The reason is that
all the differences in the descent of these Names exist
only upwards of the seventh degree, while in the seventh
and other degrees below it, all are similar. Thus in every
Name the seventh degree, and all those degrees that
are below it, descended below. But the degrees below
the seventh are not counted for they are submerged in it.

Remember that the posterior part (or progression)
of a *Havaya* is submerged in that quality of *Havaya*

which is called the anterior part. Therefore, although
the *ahurayim* (posterior parts) also descend, they are
nevertheless not counted since they are submerged. One
exception to this is the Havaya 52, which will be discussed shortly.

Something further must be borne in mind and that
is, that when there are two equal numbers, only one is
counted and not the second. Proof of this is the fact
that the ten spelled-out letters of the Name 45 fell, just
as did those of the Name 63. For when the third degree
of 45 fell, all the other degrees were drawn after it and
were submerged in it. Yet we do not count the ten
spelled-cut letters of 45, that is, the fifth degree, for this
degree is already found in the amount of 72 (Sparks) of
63. Even if the spelled-out letters of two different
Names were similar in amount, they would not both be
counted, because although the Sparks are similar in their
very being, when the lower ones fall, they remain at the
place where the upper ones had already fallen. At the
outset the ten letters of 63 descended.* Then the ten
letters of the Name 45 fell and remained at the place
where the letters of 63 were. Although they are unequal
(the ten letters of 45 being inferior to those of 63)
nevertheless when they fell below they met those of 63
and were intermingled. They fell no lower, but united
with them. This happened because they are alike in
number (each of them consisting of ten letters). How-

---

* TR. N. At the start it was the upper Kings who reigned:
and later came the reign of the the lower Kings.

ever, when numbers are dissimilar, then each individually
goes down to its appropriate place. Wherever there is
similarity, they are not repeated. The ten letters of the
Name 45 are not counted individually since they are
bound with the ten letters of the Name 63. But the
seventh degree (of the Names 72, 63, and 45) is counted
separately because in each instance it differs from the
others. The third degree of the Name 45 is counted
individually because no degree descended from the other
Names which bore any similarity to this one. Likewise,
in the Name 63 we count its 73 Sparks, that is, its fifth
degree, the ten spelled-out letters, because no similar
degree descended from the Name 72; and also the numerical value of the ten spelled-out letters, which we count
in each of the Names, because numerically all are dissimilar.

We shall now explain the fourth aggregation of 72
Sparks of the Name 52, which is "Kingdom". We have
said above that this is the fourth stage, namely the sum
of the posterior part, or progression of the simple *Havaya*,
which amounts to 72. The reason we count the posterior
part here though we do not in the other cases, is that
wherever we count the "face" or anterior part of a
Havaya, then the posterior part is completely excluded
from the count.* Thus, in the three other *Havayas*,

---

* TR. N. The eight stages earlier enumerated consist of
four pairs of Face and posterior part. Thus the first, third
fifth and seventh stages in all the Names are Face; while the
second, fourth, sixth and eighth stages are the posterior parts
of these Faces.

where we count the faces, the posterior parts submerge into the Faces and are not counted. But, here since we do not count the Face, we do count the posterior part. Yet it is necessary to know the reason why in the Name 52 the Face is not counted—if we were to count the Face then we would not have to count the posterior part, and it would be similar to the others. Therefore, it is necessary to give meaning to each stage separately.

Thus, we do not count the third stage—the sum of the four simple letters (of the Name 52, amounting to 26) because this was already included in the total of the Name 45, and is submerged in it, as mentioned earlier.

The seventh stage, or degree, which represents the amount of the spelled-out Name of 52, is not counted, although it is unlike all the other *Havayas*. Therefore, in order to understand this exclusion it is necessary to know the content of the *Havaya* 52. Of what does it consist? Note that this *Havaya* is spelled with *He's*, and is thus actually composed of two *Havayas*: in other words, it is a double *Havaya*. For the letters filling in the *Havaya* are actually the double of the simple letters. Even the *Waw* and *Dalet* that fill the *Yud*, although different in appearance from the simple Yud itself are the same in numerical value.

Of these two *Havayas* one is designated as Z'O (Microprosopus) and one as the feminine polarity. When these two are united, Z'O gives his Havaya to her and thus two Havaya's are manifested in the feminine polarity. This is the Name of 52, that of the feminine polarity.

The seventh degree of the Name 52 is not counted, for the essential part of 52 derives from Z'O and therefore we do not count it independently. For the same reason, we do not count the fifth degree either, that is, the form of the fully-spelled out letters of this Havaya. Therefore, since none of the anterior (Face) degrees could be counted, only the stage of the posterior part is counted.

It is important to know that these Names of 72 and 63 which we have already mentioned are not those which existed before the emendation took place, but rather those which came into being following the emendation. In order to understand this it is necessary to present an explanation, as follows.

When the ten Points issued from the eyes of Adam Kadmon, and were traversing the world of Emanation in their descent to the world of Creation, they left their impressions there. From the Points of their Crown the *Parezuf* Microprosopus, or Crown, was later made.* From the Points of their "Wisdom" and "Intelligence", the *Parezufim* of Father and Mother (which are "Wisdom" and "Intelligence" in the world of Emanation) were made following the emendation. And from the Points of their seven lower *Sefirot*, the *Parezufim* of ZO'N, which are the seven *Sefirot* of Emanation, were later made. (ZO'N comprises Microprosopus and his Feminine Polarity.)

---

* TR. N. This is the *Parezuf* of *Arik Anpin*.

However later, at the time of emendation, the worlds descended from their original degrees and they were not located as they had been at first, but in a different manner, as follows. It has been shown that the seven lower *Sefirot* of Macroprosopus are enclothed in the world of Emanation, and as will be shown later, that all the *Parezufim* clothe him. From this, it would seem to be fitting that Father and Mother, which represent "Wisdom" and "Intelligence", should abide above, at the place of "Wisdom" and "Intelligence" of Macroprosopus —but this was not the case. Instead, they enclothed "Mercy" and "Power" of Macroprosopus.

The same condition obtains with Z'O, Microprosopus, which consists of the six lower *Sefirot*. In like manner, they should have enclothed the six *Sefirot* of Macroprosopus, but this was not the case. Instead, they clothed only from half of its *Sefira* "Beauty" on down. But "Kingdom" remained in its first position and enfolded "Kingdom" of Macroprosopus.

Summarizing the foregoing, we shall say that the Name 72, whose place is in "Wisdom", enfolded "Mercy". The Name 63, whose place is in "Intelligence", enfolded only "Power" of *Arik Anpin*. The Name 45, which is synonymous with Z'O was placed at the lower half of "Beauty" and "Triumph", "Glory" and "Foundation" of Macroprosopus, although Z'O itself comprises all of six *Sefirot*. And the Name 52 is in "Kingdom" itself, for "Kingdom" alone remained in its place.

It is evident then that the Names 72 and 63 mentioned above are not those Names which existed prior to the emendation, but those that exist following the emendation. In other words, the Names 72 and 63 to which we ascribe shattering were those entities which following the Emendation, were fit to clothe "Mercy" and "Power" of Macroprosopus. If this were not the case and they had remained in the form of the original entities, it would have been impossible for the Names 72 and 63 to have undergone shattering, particularly since it is known that these two Names represent "Wisdom" and "Intelligence", the two *Sefirot* that have never undergone shattering.

It is essential to understand that these 288 Sparks (R'P'H) are all very severe Judgments. They issued from the Primordial "Kings" that were shattered; these "Kings" in turn were issued from the "strong Light" (*Butzino Decordenuso*) which was hidden in the womb of the Mother (Intelligence)—as expressed in the *Zohar*. This "strong Light" is the origin of all the Judgments and Judicial Powers. Because it resides in Mother she is designated as the source of all Judgments. The *Zohar* also notes that Judgments arise from her. It is this Light which fixes the measure and limit of every *Sefira*.

Note that since she is the source of all Judgments, this act of limiting is ascribed to her. This is because every measure and limit to things is the result of Judgment, whose nature it is to restrain. This is closely related to the nature of the husks or shells—the *Kelipah*.

Bear in mind that "Mercy" (*Hesed*) and "Justice" (*Din*) are the two stages created by the Supreme Emanator for the purpose of governing the world. They are of diverse nature. The nature of "Mercy" is to extend amply, without limit or measure, whereas the nature of

"Justice" is to conceal the Light and to completely restrain it. However, in ño instance does one of these two
attributes act independently of the other. Thus there
is no Mercy without Justice and no Justice without
Mercy. The root of the matter lies in this: Mercy's
nature is to flow forth, to extend itself, while that of
Justice is to restrain. But while Justice is still close to
its sources, it cannot entirely fulfill its function because
of the strength of the Light of the source, the Infinite,
blessed be He. Because of this, Mercy triumphs greatly
over Justice. As, however, the descent below proceeds
and the source becomes more remote, the Light of Mercy
is decreased and the power of Justice is increased. In
this manner, it proceeds from stage to stage, the Light
becoming ever smaller and Justice ever increasing until
there remains only Justice, entirely without Mercy. At
this point Justice restrains and entirely blocks the Light;
here it is called "husk" or "shell", or "rigid and severe
Justice". This sort of Justice is unfit to abide in the
Divine Realm and is expelled below. It is called "scum"
because it is actually the sediment of Justice.

Let us now examine the origin and development of
Justice. We have already declared at the outset that
before anything existed in the world, it was necessary
that the Supreme Emanator conceal His Light so that it
would not be extended in its full might. That act already
marked the beginning of the manifestation of the root
of Justice. Although the use of the term "Justice" is
inappropriate in such an exalted realm, nevertheless, since
there was a kind of "hindering" of the Light, the source,
or origin of Justice took root here. Therefore, the

starting-point of existence for the root of Justice occurred at the first contraction of the Light. But there it absolutely did not manifest, because of the exalted nature of the realm. Only when it extended below did Justice increase in power. Thus, in each and every world the Light is diminished and Justice increases in power until it becomes so rigid that it cannot abide in the Divine realm, and is thus expelled. It is called *"sitra ahara"* (the "other side"), or the extreme opposite of the Divine Light. This "other side" is a different creation, opposed in nature to the Divine *Sefirot*. In short, it is the essence of the "husk". Further details about the nature of the husks will be dealt with in later chapters.

Chapter Seven

The "Strong Light" is the root of all the Judgments. From her issue the "Kings", which are composed of the substance of these extremely severe Judgments. As it is said in the *Idra* portion of the *Zohar;* "A Spark brought forth Sparks, and the number of Sparks scattered is 320." In other words, these Sparks that issued from the Strong Light, were divided into 320, and constituted the seven "Kings" which broke. The Judgments residing within Mother are the *Butsino* or "Strong" Lights, they are comprised of 320 Sparks, for five times *"Din"* (Judgment) whose numerical value is 64 amounts to 320. From these, the "Kings" issued, but they constitute only 315, lacking five. These five are the origin from which all of them were issued and spread into 7 x 45 (the number of Adam.

The reason for this is that those seven "Kings" are Z'O in whom there is a *Havaya* (Holy Name) with *Alef,* the numerical value of which is 45, equalling Adam. For the past reason they are seven times "Adam" (45)—amounting to 315.

Nevertheless, because they originate from the 320 Judgments of Mother, they are spread out into 320 Sparks in the following manner. There are really eight "Kings" in all. Each is divided into four, after the manner of the four-lettered *Havaya.* As we have pointed out above, the Lights of the world of Emanation are all

Havayas. Thus, we find that since four times eight is thirty-two, and each of these thirty-two comprises ten (for it is known that each *Sefira* comprises ten *Sefirot*) they total 320, for 10 x 32 is 320.

At the time of the selection and emendation only 288 Sparks in all were selected. The remaining Sparks were left in Mother and are called "thorns". In the future, at the coming of the Messiah the Owner of the Orchard will come and destroy these thorns. They will vanish from the face of the earth. As it is said in the Scriptures: "And I will take away the stony heart". (Ezekiel XXVI, 26). It must be understood that the thorns are 32 in number, the same as the numerical value of the word *lev* (heart). This touches on the mystery of the "stone heart". The Creator made His promise for the future to eliminate the 32 thorns from the world.

The reason for the selection of only 288 Sparks is that in each path "Kingdom" could not be selected, for it is the lowest of all the entities and nearest to the shell or husk. Only the three primary *Sefirot,* and the six succeeding Ones of every entity were selected. Thus we get 288 Sparks in all; from this number, Sparks are constantly being selected which rise above to the Divine Realm. These 288 Sparks are the total of four quantities of 72 Sparks that fell from above. Later, at the time of emendation, when the Kings rose up to Mother to be emended, she gave them a drop of M'N (the Feminine Waters) which comprises *five* Judgments, and thereby completed them at the number 320, for they were originally 315 in number. Later they became 325, that is, through the union of Father and Mother, when he gave her five Judgments.   In her newly tempered state they become five Mercies; through these Mercies the 320 Sparks are tempered, or sweetened, and become 325.

In the words of the *Zohar*: "We have learned that from the "Strong Light" issue 325 Sparks." That is to say, after they are tempered by the Judgments of Father, they issue as the number of 325.

To reiterate: at the outset the "Kings" were issued from the *five* Judgments that are within Mother. These "Kings" are the 320 Judgments, which we compute by multiplying *Din*—64—by five. Later, they decrease in number to 315, which is equivalent to seven times Adam —45. At the time of the emendation, they regain their original number of 320 because of the drop of M'N— feminine waters—with which Mother completes them. They are subsequently tempered by the Judgments of Father ("Wisdom"), which turn to Mercies in Mother, and become 325.

It is important to know also that in the Feminine Polarity there are 320 Judgments, this total (320) being arrived at by multiplying *Din* (Judgment), or 64, by 5. This distinguishes her as "Rigid Judgment" in the aspect of the seven "Kings". Later, when the Masculine Polarity unites with her, they become 325.

It is important to understand this concept thoroughly, for by five times *Din* we mean that *Din* which derives from the Holy Name *ADNI*, and adds up to a total of 320.

At that point the Judgments are absolutely untempered. But when the five *Alefs* which are the five Names of *AHW'H* unite with them they become tempered, and reach the number 325: Specifically five times *ADNI* (whose number is 65), or 325.

The Feminine Polarity is then called "the virgin" (*naaroh*—which also has the numerical value of 325) who receives the masculine essence. In other words, after she receives the modification of five Judgments from the Masculine Polarity, she also becomes fit to receive the drop of Mercies. Because of this modification, or tempering which the Feminine Polarity receives from the Masculine Polarity, she is called, in the words of the *Zohar*, "Mild Judgment". For she herself is rigid Judgment, but through the conjoining of the Masculine with her (that is, of the five *Alefs* from the Name *AHY'H*) her Judgments are tempered. As a result, she is designated "Mild Judgment".

It is necessary to note that this addition of "five" which the Masculine Polarity gives the Feminine Polarity in order to temper her Judgments, are the five Judgments called "M'N'Z'P'K" (the five final Hebrew letters) the numerical value of which is 280. It is through these five that her Judgments are tempered.

Remember that the 320 are the Judgments of the Feminine Polarity alone, where as the Judgments of "M'N'Z'P'K" belong to the Male Polarity alone. He transfers them to the *Sefira* "Foundation" (*Yesod*) of the Feminine Polarity.

The foregoing should thoroughly explain the idea of the 288 Sparks, as well as the meanings of the 320 and the 325 Judgments mentioned many times in the *Zohar* and elsewhere as the "Kings" which are in the nature of Judgments, and which were later tempered and emended in their places.

Chapter

Eight

Up to now we have depicted that which pertains to the world of *Nekudot*, the "chaotic world." In the following pages we shall explain the subject of the "*Olam ha-Berudim*" the Emended World, and the order of the *Parezufim* of the world of Emanation, as they were arranged by the Supreme Emanator.

After the worlds were disintegrated, and had descended from their original stages, the Supreme Emanator issued the New Name 45 (*Mah ha-Hodosh*) through which everything was emended. In order to issue this Name, the two Names 72 and 63 of Adam Kadmon united again, and thus the New Name 45 was brought to birth. It was issued from the forehead of Adam Kadmon. It was not actually new, but was now renewed by the power of the Light of the union of the Names 72 and 63.

This Name, 45, raised up all the extractions from the husks, and combined them into pillars; for what actually had caused the disintegration was the arrangement of the "Kings" one below the other without anything linking them together. But now, being united as pillars, they were able to continue to exist.

After raising the shell extractions that are of the quality of the Name 52, the new Name, 45, united with them; it is considered to be the Masculine Polarity, while the Name 52 is the Feminine Polarity.   (Every *Sefira* was comprised of male and female.)

A portion of Sparks still remained among the husks. By means of our daily prayers we gradually raise them, until eventually they will all be raised to their proper realm.   Then the husks will be left without sustenance, and will therefore be lifeless.   At this point they will completely vanish.   This will occur in the future, at the advent of Messiah, when, as the Prophet expresses it: "He will destroy death forever." (Isaiah XXV).

Now let us examine the process of emendation in detail.   When the Supreme Emenator desired that the worlds which had been rendered defective should be emended, He brought forth the New Name 45, which issued from the Forehead of Adam Kadmon, and united with the Name 52, in order to correct the creation.

However, to fully understand the emendation, we must investigate the nature of this new Name 45, and the manner in which it became united with the Name called 52.   The Name 45 comprises ten *Sefirot,* and is divided into four categories, namely: T'N'T'O (or *Ta'* amim, Nekudot, *T*agin and Otiot).   This is also true of the Name 52.   When the *Sefirot* of 45 and 52 unite, then together they are designated as ten complete *Sefirot,* since they comprise both Masculine and Feminine qualities.

TA'AMIM (signs indicating pitch) are Intelligence
NEKUDOT (vowel sounds)   „ Crown
TAGIN (ornamental strokes)   „ Wisdom
OTIOT (letters)   ” Microprosopus
          and his Feminine Polarity

However, their subdivision in *Parezufim* is not in accordance with the above arrangement. Nor do the *Sefirot*
of 45 and 52 correspond to each other: that is, for example, "Crown" of 45 does not match with Crown of
52, "Wisdom" of 45 does not match with "Wisdom" of
52, and so on. Instead their order is as follows:

The two *Parezufim* of *Atik* and *Arik* together constitute "Crown" of the world of Emanation. Thus *Atik*
took for himself all of the Crown of 45, which are the
Ta'amim; half of the Crown of 52, which are his first
five *Sefirot;* the first three *Sefirot* of "Wisdom" of 52;
the first four *Sefirot* of "Intelligence": and the seven
"Crowns" of the seven lower *Sefirot* of 52. *Arik* took
for himself all of "Wisdom" of 45, which are the *Nekudot,* and half of "Crown" of 52, that is, from his *Sefira*
Beauty downward.

Father took to himself half of "Intelligence" of 45,
(which are the *Tagin*), and the seven lower Sefirot of
"Wisdom", for her first three had been taken by *Atik.*

Mother took to herself the lower half of "Intelligence" of 45, which are the *Tagin,* and the six lower
Sefirot of "Intelligence" of 52, for the four upper ones
had been taken by *Atik.*

The seven lower *Sefirot* took to themselves the
seven lower *Sefirot* of the names 45 and 52, excluding,
however, the seven Crowns of the seven lower *Sefirot* of
52, which remained in *Atik.*

Do not conclude that the *Parezufim* are one thing,
and what they have taken is something else, for this is
not so. The truth is that the *Parezufim* that were constructed here are themselves the substance of the *Sefirot*
of 45 and 52, in the order outlined above.

Bear in mind that that which the *Parezufim* took from the Name 45 is masculine, while that from 52 is feminine. For instance, the part which *Atik* took from 45 is designated "Male *Atik*" and that taken from 52 is designated "Female *Atik*." The same is true in the case of *Arik Anpin*.

Do not question the presence in such exalted realms —which are all Compassion—of the Feminine Polarity, which is Judgment. From the words of the *Zohar*, too, it is seen that the Feminine Polarity was revealed only from the *Parezufim* of Father and Mother downward. In fact, as stated previously, the main objective of the emendation of every entity is that it shall constitute both Masculine and Feminine Polarities. Thus we find that the *Parezuf* of *Atik* is constituted of 45 and 52. However, this does not signify that the Feminine Polarity of *Atik* is a Parezuf distinct from him. This is impossible, for the reason above mentioned. However, when we speak of the "Feminine Polarity of *Atik*" we merely mean the feminine essence found in this *Parezuf*, namely the essence of the Name 52.

The same is true of the *Parezuf* of *Arik*. But this is not the case with Father and Mother or Microprospus and his Feminine Polarity; here the Feminine Polarities are *Parezufim* different from the masculine, and comprising both Names 45 and 52—just as does the Masculine Polarity.

You must understand that the emendation of the *Parezufim* corresponded to the extent of the specific defect which had been incurred in them. Thus, in *Atik*, in whom there was no defect whatsoever, the emendation effected absolute unity in him. This means that 45 and 52 became one *Parezuf* and only the Face was visible in them. However the Name 52, in relation to 45, is called the "posterior".

In *Arik* also there was no trace whatsoever of annulment. Therefore his Feminine Polarity was emended by being completely united with him, although not in exactly the same way as in *Atik*. The masculine part here was arranged on the right and the feminine on the left. In other words, 45, which is the masculine, is at his right, and 52, which is the feminine, is at his left. In the case of *Atik*, this was not so, for both right and left sides comprised 45 and 52. The reason for this difference is that here in *Arik* the posterior part of his last three *Sefirot*— "Triumph" "Glory" and "Foundation"— were defective.

Since Father and Mother had suffered annulment in their posterior parts, they are considered as two absolutely distinct *Parezufim*. But because this defect had affected only their posterior parts, they are perpetually "face to face", and their union is constant.

In ZO'N (the six lower *Sefirot*—Z'O and "Kingdom", or *Nukbah*, the Feminine Polarity) shattering did occur involving defect in both the Face and the posterior parts. That is why they issued as two separate *Parezufim*, entirely severed from each other; that is, they issued "back to back" with a single wall or partition between both. In order to arrange them face to face it is necessary to saw through the partition, and to separate them. The act of "sawing through" will be explained shortly.

There may be some questions about *Atik* and *Arik*, for how can we speak of union when neither of them is severed from its Feminine Polarity? The matter is as follows. The Names 45 and 52 united to build one *Parezuf*, which is called *Atik*. Their posterior parts consist of Lights which do not shine very brightly, due to the fact that they are of the essence of Judgment, which is submerged within. The substance that does shine is of the essence of Mercy and it is *this* that is revealed. Thus the whole *Parezuf* of *Atik* is found to be nothing but anterior, or face, and it has no back or posterior part whatsoever. This, you will recall, is also true of the *Sefira* "Foundation".

The only discrimination to be made in the *Parezuf Atik* is that the Name 45 is designated male and the Name 52 is designated female. This applies to *Parezuf Atik* alone. In *Arik* the arrangement is different. Here the Names 45 and 52 are united, making one *Parezuf*, *which* is called *Arik Anpin* (Macroprosopus) only 45 is set at the right and 52 at the left. Thus, we find that 45 is a complete *Parezuf* in itself, as is 52. One is designated "male" and the other "female". But both as one are called *Parezuf Arik Anpin*.

The Name 45, in relation to every *Parezuf* is considered as the right side pillar in the same way that Z'O repressnts the six lower *Sefirot* in relation to the entire world of emanation.

Chapter Nine

The following is a detailed explanation of how the *Parezufim* were emended, beginning with *Atik*, the first to undergo the change. A brief recapitulation of the differences between a *Nekuda* (Point), a *Sefira* and a *Parezuf*, is in order at this point.

We have already established that all created beings are characterized by a four-fold division (corresponding to the four letters of the Holy Name *Havaya*, from which all originates). And just as there are four worlds: *Azilut, Beriah, Yezirah* and *Asiah,* so every part of them must necessarily comprise these four categories. And only when they do so are they considered to be complete. Thus, when we speak of a "Point", to indicate *Asiah* alone, we are referring to something which comprises five *Parezufim,* each of which in turn comprises ten *Sefirot.* When we speak of a "Sefira" we refer to that which comprises the four worlds, of which each constitutes five *Parezufim* of ten *Sefirot* each. And when we speak of a "Parezuf" we mean ten *Sefirot,* which comprise the four worlds, each of which comprises the five *Parezufim* that comprise ten *Sefirot* each.

Something further is required for a *Parezuf* to be designated as complete: namely, that all ten individual *Sefirot* within the particular *Sefira* that is being made into a *Parezuf*, shall shine. Through the power of these illuminations, the number of the members of the body of the *Parezuf* attains to 613. Furthermore, *Keter*, the "Crown", makes up the Head, and its Lights are concealed. *Hokmah*, "Wisdom", radiates ten illuminations, as follows:

WISDOM

WISDOM AND INTELLIGENCE	—the two eyes
KNOWLEDGE	—the forehead
MERCY and POWER	—the two temples of the forehead
BEAUTY	—the bridge of the nose
TRIUMPH and GLORY	—the two ears
FOUNDATION	—the tip of the nose
KINGDOM	—the two nostrils

"Intelligence" also emanated ten Lights, from which the *Sefirot* of the mouth were effected. A detailed description follows:

INTELLIGENCE

WISDOM AND INTELLIGENCE	—palate and throat
MERCY and POWER	—two sets of gums upper and lower
TRIUMPH and GLORY	—the two lips
the entire middle pillar— (KNOWLEDGE, BEAUTY and FOUNDATION)	—tongue
KINGDOM	—mouth

Similarly each and every *Sefira* emitted its illuminations according to the manner decreed by the wisdom of the Emanator. An these illuminations together comprise a total of 613, designating a complete *Parezuf* (Person).

Since we said earlier that from the eyes, ears, nose and mouth, issued the four senses (seeing, hearing, smell and speech) and that these represent respectively: "Wisdom", "Intelligence", "Beauty" and "Kingdom", you may question how we conclude that Intelligence issues from the ears if they were made from the *Sefirot of* "Wisdom". The same question may arise in connection with the nose and the mouth, and their *Sefirot*. The matter is as follows: The features of the face were effected through the extension of the *Sefirot* of "Wisdom", but these four vehicles of sense were issued from the Holy Name *Havaya*, which resided in the interior and thereby emanated to the exterior at the places where it found openings. The *Yud* found the apertures of the eyes and spread forth through that path, where it bacame the sense of sight. The *He* found the openings of the ears and issued there, becoming the sense of hearing; the *Waw* issued through the openings of the nose and became the sense of smell, and the final *He'* issued through the mouth and became the sense of speech.

There are therefore two distinct matters under consideration: the *features*, which were fashioned from the *Sefirot* "Wisdom" and "Intelligence", and the senses, which were fashioned from the *Havaya* that resided in the interior. By means of its passing through the features, the senses came into existence. If it were not for this passing Light the features would exist without the senses. This indicates that the features constitute one subject and the senses another, one having nothing at all to do with the other. It must be remembered that these terms are all highly symbolic. The names assigned to them refer to the branches which issue from them; and these are nothing but the Light of the Infinite Himself, extended in such a manner as to allow nothing to exist below that did not have its root in the Upper Sources. This arrangement assures the existence and sustenance of the branches.

Now let us return to the matter of the individual *Parezufim*. We shall start with *Atik*, the first one. *Parezuf Atik* is above the world of Emanation, that is, it is not a part of that world. Nevertheless it is enfolded in it, as we shall explain. This *Atik* is made from "Kingdom" of Adam Kadmon, and comprises both masculine and feminine polarities that is, the Names 45 and 52. The "Kingdom" here referred to is none other than the *Sefira* "Kingdom" of the Infinite World, and is therefore above the world of Emanation. In previous discussion we have described how "Kingdom" of each world is enclosed within the next world below it, and how it is equivalent in dimension to the entire world that succeeds it. In this way, all the worlds are bound one within the other until finally that point is reached where everything is bound up with the Emanator.

It is necessary to know that the masculine polarity of *Atik*, namely the essence of the Name 45, which is in him, is not enfolded within the world of Emanation at all. Because of its high degree of concealment, it is totally imperceptible. Only the feminine polarity of

Atik is enfolded, but even of her only the seven lower *Sefirot* are enfolded. The three topmost *Sefirot* remain bare and are completely imperceptible. They are designated as the "Unknown Head" because of the many uncertainties surrounding them. This has been fully explained elsewhere, and require no further elaboration.*

The manner of enclothement of the seven *Sefirot* is as follows:

SEVEN SEFIROT OF ATIK			WORLD OF EMANATION
MERCY of ATIK	enclothed in		CROWN OF ARIK (Macroprosopus)
POWER	"	"	WISDOM
BEAUTY	"	"	INTELLIGENCE
Upper parts	"	"	
TRIUMPH and GLORY	"	"	MERCY and POWER
Middle parts of	"	"	
TRIUMPH and GLORY	"	"	TRIUMPH and GLORY
The lower parts of	"	"	

TRIUMPH and GLORY descended to KINGDOM of ARIK and became there like two breasts bestowing bounty to the worlds. FOUNDATION is divided into two sections only:

* See Chapter III.

SEVEN SEFIROT

OF ATIK	WORLD OF EMANATION
Upper part of	
FOUNDATION enclothed in	BEAUTY
Lower part of	
FOUNDATION " "	FOUNDATION
KINGDOM " "	KINGDOM OF
	AZILUT
	(Emanation)

The World of Emanation comprises five *parezufim*, which are as follows:

1) ARIK   (Macroprosopus)
2) ABA   (Father)
3) IMA   (Mother)
4) Z'O (Six Sefirot from "Mercy" to "Foundation")
5) NUKA   (KINGDOM)

The first *Parezuf* is *Arik*, and he pervades all the *Parezufim* to the point where his "Kingdom" is enclothed in "Kingdom" of the World of Emanation. He is chief of all the *Parezufim*, and the others are no more than branches which issue from him. He is the one *Parezuf* that extends from the very beginning of the world of Emanation down to its end, and all the other *Parezufim* ramify from him in the following way. From the throat to the navel, he is enclothed in *Aba* and *Ima*; *Aba* enclothes his right side, *Ima* his left. From the navel downward, he is enclothed in Z'O and Nukba.

Just as *Arik* pervades all the *Parezufim*, so do all the other *Parezufim* pervade each other, from the point in them which is called Beauty, downward, so that all end evenly. This is in accordance with the rule that one *Sefira* from a higher world is as large as the entire world that follows it. The same principle applies to the individual *Parezufim*. Thus, one *Sefira* of an upper *Parezuf* is as large as three *Sefirot* of the next consecutive *Parezuf*. We find then that all the *Parezufim* clothe each other, and are bound together as one, their source being *Arik Anpin*.

Arik is "Crown" of the world of Emanation. His Lights were extended to the point where a *Parezuf* was constructed. In this *Parezuf* there is one point of difference from the other *Parezufim*, namely: In the head of all the other *Parezufim* there are three types of Brain—"Wisdom", "Intelligence" and "Knowledge", with "Knowledge" comprising "Mercies" and Powers". But in this *Parezuf* only one type of brain is to be found in the Head—that of its *Sefira* "Wisdom". For "Intelligence" has descended into the throat, and "Knowledge" to a place between the shoulder blades.

The brain of the *Sefira* "Wisdom" is called the "sealed brain", for it is closed and cannot be grasped at all. It is spoken of as "wine which is still and undisturbed above its sediment" because it is comprised of absolute clarity and purity and has no admixture whatsoever.

Chapter

Ten

The topic of the three heads mentioned in the *Zohar*—"Three heads are carved out, one within the other, each above the other", is an important one. As mentioned earlier, the first three *Sefirot* of *Atik's* feminine polarity, were not enclothed in *Arik*, remaining bare and uncovered. They are designated by the title "the Unknown Head" because this head is concealed and totally inconceivable. This head remained above that of *Arik*, encircling it, and is but the first of the three heads. Of it the *Idra* of the *Zohar* says: "It is the head of all the heads; it is a head which is not a head; it does not know and it is not known".

The second head is "Crown" of *Arik*. It is the white cranium mentioned earlier, which is called: "the upper head, the holy ancient *Atika Kadishoh*, the concealed of all the concealed ones".

The third head is "Wisdom" of *Arik*. It is the concealed brain, of which the *Zohar* says: "one head, the hidden Wisdom, which is veiled, etc. . . .". However, there is another enumeration of three heads. Although "Crown" and "Wisdom" are but two heads, nevertheless they are divided into three, and these are called "the three Heads of *Arik*", for they all are actually *of* him. The air between "Crown" and "Intelligence" of *Arik*, and "Knowledge" of *Atik* is hidden, and is designated

as "tenuous air" (awira dahyia). This is an apt designa-
tion since it is also called the "upper concealed brain".
It is considered as one head, the second of the three heads
of *Arik*.

Thus, when we say "three heads", we are referring
to "Crown", "Wisdom" and "Intelligence" of the feminine polarity of *Atik*, which remained unclad. "Crown"
and "Wisdom" of *Arik*, are each designated by this
name of "head", and when we speak of the "three heads
of *Arik*", we are not considering the three heads of the
feminine polarity of *Atik*, since they are not a part of
Arik's body. *Arik's* three heads are as follows:

1) Crown
2) Knowledge of Atik—located between Crown and
   Wisdom
3) Wisdom

In speaking of the shattering of the vessels, we explained why there are two grades of "three heads", and
the source from which they ar drawn. Now we shall
proceed to explain this matter of the three heads of *Arik*
and the emendation which they effect in detail.

There are only two heads, namely "Crown" and
"Wisdom", of *Arik*, but they are considered as three
because of "Knowledge" of *Atik*, which is hidden be-
tween them. It is important to know that each of these
three heads of Arik contains in itself three *Havayas* and
One, the Superstructure, as it were, that comprises them.
There is a difference in the spelled-out letters of the
Names in the different heads; that is, those which are in
"Crown" are spelled with *Yuds*, and have a numerical

value of 72; those which are in the *Awira* (the second
head) and have the spelling of the Name 63 (the letter
waw is here spelled with an *alef* instead of with a yud;
and those of the third head, "Wisdom", spelled with
alef's and yielding a numerical value of 45.

In each of these three heads there are three *Havayas*,
with a total of twelve letters. Together with the container which encompasses them, there are thirteen. From
each of these an emendation is effected. Namely, from
the thirteen found in the head which is designated "air",
thirteen "niemen" are executed. These are the hairs of
this particular head. The *Idra* speaks of them as follows:
"There are thirteen *niemen* of the hair, which are found
to exist on either side." The order of their division is
as follows:

4 on the right side of the head
4 on the left side of the head
4 on the nape of the neck
1 in the center of the head.

This last comprises all the others. These hairs are white,
for anything black is considered to partake of Judgment.
But here, because there is no Judgment they are white.

In Z'O it is different. There Judgment does function and the hair is black. There is a further difference
between the heads of Z'O and that of *Arik Anpin* for in
Z'O' the hairs intermingle, whereas in *Arik Anpin* they
are all separate from each other. As the Zohar expresses
it: "It is like pure wool whose strands are not interwoven." The hair is long, extending to the shoulder,
and it is not rigid like those of the beard, for it is de-

signed to bestow bounty through its openings. Therefore it is long and soft, and quite different from the hair
of the beard, which will be described later.

From the thirteen letters which are in the cranium
(gulgalte) thirteen white areas (hivruti) are established
between the hairs. "His white cranium shines in the
thirteen carved paths," says the *Idra*. These paths are
divided in the same way as the hair, that is:

4 on the right side
4 on the left side
4 on the nape of the neck
1 in the center, which encompasses them all.

Those at the nape of the neck extend down below into
Z'O so as to complete his beard, and supply it with
thirteen emendations. These hairs surround and cover
the face; they are short and rigid, because they have the
quality of Judgment, and being the containers of Compassion as well as Judgment, they are called the "thirteen
compartments of Compassion".

The Emanator designed them for the purpose of
enabling the bounty to descend within measured limits
so that it can be received by the nether beings. It is
through these "Compartments of Compassion" that the
husks are subdued, for it is known that the sacred
Powers vanquish the husks.

The beard is fashioned by "Concealed Wisdom" in
which Power of *ATIK* is found to be enclothed. When
this beard shines forth, its Light subdues the husks.

The detail pertaining to the thirteen emendations of
the beard will be presented in the following chapter.

Chapter
Eleven

To continue our discussion of the three heads, note that in each of them are found both substance and vessels, that is, inner content and outer content. In each of *these* are to be found three distinct types of essences, namely:

1) the inner essence
2) the outer essence which encircles the first
3) the outermost essence which encircles the second

Everything of divine content comprises these three essences. In this way Crown, which is the first of the three heads, possesses these three essences, both in its substance and in its vessels. In the three essences of the substance there are three *Havayas*—spelled out with *Yud's*—which give a numerical value of 72. The difference between them is in the vowels. In the interior essence, the vowel is only placed under the initial four letters of the *Havaya,* and accords with the sound (movement) of the letter. Thus, the *Yud* has a *holam* (.), *He'* has a *zera* (..), Waw has a komez (T), and the final He' has also a *zera* (..). In the encircling Light, the

spelled-out letter are also vowelled like the simple letters; but in the outermost encircling Light, the initial letters are vowelled like the others, while the
spelled-out letters are vowelled throughout with a *komez*.
In the three essences of the vessels there are three Names,
AKY'K, all spelled with *Yud's* with the numerical value
of 161, and vowelled in the same manner as the *Havayas*
mentioned above.

The foregoing is a specific description, but in general all three essences of the "Crown", in relation to the
others, are no more than the encircling Light which sur-
rounds all the other encircling Lights.

In the three qualities of essence of the second head—
that of "air" (*awira*)—there are three *Havayas*, each
with a numerical value of 63.   They are vowelled like
those of Crown.   However, the difference is that wherever in Crown there was a letter vowelled with *komez*
here it is vowelled with a *patah* (—).

In the vessels there are found three Holy Names,
AHY'H spelled with *Yud's* and vowelled in the same
manner as the *Havayas*.   All three essences of the head of
"Air" are nothing but an encircling Light in relation to
the others.

In the three qualities of essence of the substance of
"Concealed Wisdom" (the third Head) are found three
Havayas, spelled with *Alef's* and having a numerical
value of 45.   They are vowelled in the same manner as
we have described relating to air, but wherever there is
a *zera* in *Awira*, here a *segol* (.·.) replaces it.   The vessels have three Names, AHY'H, spelled with *Alef's* that
bear a numerical value of 143.   The arrangement of the

vowels here is the same as in the *Havayas*. These three qualities are considered to be the inner Light in relation to the others.

The three heads are, collectively, three entities, as follows:

1) "Crown" (*Kitra*) which encompasses the encircling Light
2) "Air" (*Awira*) which is the encircling Light
3) "Concealed Wisdom" (*Hokmah Stimoe* which is the inner Light

Yet each head individually comprises all three entities, as explained above. "Crown" and "Brain", enfold each other. This is referred to in the Idra: "One is within the other."

Now let us turn to the seven lower *Sefirot* of the head. They are seven emendations which are found in the head of *Arik,* designated as:

1) GULGATE HIVRE   (the white cranium)
2) TALE' DIBEDULHA   (the crystalline dew)
3) KERUMA' DE-AWIRA   (the tegument of the air)
4) RAAWA' D' RAAWIN   (will of Wills*)
5) 'AMOR NOKIY   (the pure wool)
6) PEKIHU DE'AYENIN   (the opening of the eyes)
7) HUTMA'   (the nose)

---

*This refers to the highest "will to good".

The Acrostic G'T'K'R'A'P'H is an aid in remember-
ing them. It has already been pointed out that the
seven lower *Sefirot* of *Atik* were enclothed in *Arik,* and
that from these, seven emendations of the head were
effected as follows:

1) THE WHITE CRANIUM. This is made from
"Mercy" of *Atik,* which was enclothed in it. It is
called "white" because of the Mercy inherent in it. Since
the cranium is its place, it follows that this "Mercy" is
the source of all the *Sefirot* "Mercies", in addition to
being the beginning of the masculine polarity of *Arik,*
for the right side of *Arik* is masculine.

2) THE CRYSTALLINE DEW. This is the "Concealed
Wisdom", whose name, *tal* ("dew"), is actually the first
three letters of the *Havaya*—Y'H'W—which is brain.
The word "crystalline" is attached because "Power" of
Atik is enclothed in it. For "Wisdom" itself is the right
pillar and "Power" is the left; therefore the dew is
called "crystalline" because all the colors are visible in
the bounty which comprises both "Mercy" and "Judgment". Because "Power" is enclothed in *Atik,* "Concealed Wisdom" becomes the source of all the "Powers",
so much so that all measures and limits are drawn from it.

3) THE TEGUMENT OF THE AIR, was made from
"Beauty" of *Atik* and this particular emendation effects
a twofold improvement. First, it hovers over the "Concealed Wisdom" so that the hidden Light of "Knowledge"
of *Atik,* shall not shine too powerfully there. This will
be elaborated on later. Second, it prevents the Light of
"Concealed Wisdom" from descending too powerfully
to the nether beings, and thus enables them to bear it.

4) THE WILL OF WILLS. This is made by "Foundation" of *Atik*, which shines in the forehead of *Arik*. It is for this reason that the forehead of *Arik* differs from any forehead that is below it. For those lower ones are in the nature of Judgment. When they are revealed, all the Judgments are stirred up—whereas *Arik's* forehead, because it is tempered by "Foundation" of *Atik* which is revealed in it, is called the "forehead of the Will" to compassion which sweetens (and tempers) all the Judgments below. This action is continual, even when it is covered with hair. However, when it is unveiled, all the Judgments are subdued and are rendered totally ineffective. This is a time when the Supreme Will is abundantly revealed, for everything is tempered by the Light of this forehead. Yet, because the worlds are in need of Judgment the unveiling of the forehead is not continuous, and occurs only at intervals.

5) THE PURE WOOL. This is made by those parts of "Triumph" and "Glory" of *Atik* that are above "Foundation." Passing through the head, "Triumph" and "Glory" effect the emendation in that the hair that has issued from the "Concealed Wisdom", is here drawn below and acts like a group of channels which perform certain tasks.

Here the power of "Triumph" and "Glory", which symbolize two *Waw's* (extended lines) provides the impetus for all this. As a result, the hair appears in the form of lines like the letter *Waw*. Being white, like natural wool, it is called "pure wool".

6) THE OPENING OF THE EYES, is made by those parts of "Triumph" and "Glory" which are below

"Foundation" of *Atik*. Note that the emendation of the
"pure wool", which is made by the portions of "Triumph" and "Glory" of *Atik* which are above "Foundation", is higher than the forehead, where an emendation
was made by "Foundation", and that this latter emendation is below the forehead, since it is made from the
parts below "Foundation".   When the Lights pass
through the head, they effect this emendation, for the
eyes were already put there, when the particular *Sefirot*
of "Wisdom" passed through.   The purpose of this
emendation is to enable them to exist without a curtain,
free from any cover, so that they may ever be open to
watch over the nether beings.   Of this effect, the *Zohar*
states: "An open eye that does not slumber; no cover,
no eyelid, is upon the eye".   And in the same connection
there is a verse in the Psalms: "Behold he that keepeth
Israel shall neither slumber nor sleep."   (Psalm 121).
Eyelids restrain the light of the eyes, and since you already
know that anything which restrains is of the nature of
Judgment, nothing exists in these eyes to restrain their
Light, for they are very much "sweetened"—or tempered.
In addition, it was necessary for these eyes to be forever
open so that the permanent existence of the *Sefirot* be
assured through the continued presence of God's bounty.

Note that although we express "eyes" in the plural,
denoting two eyes, a right and a left, nevertheless since
they are in *Arik*—a place wehrein there cannot possibly
be any trace of Judgment—they are considered to be
but one: and this a right eye, for the left is not counted.
As the *Idra* puts it: "There is no left in this *Atika*." These
eyes are different from those below, for down there colors

are discernible in them. They are of scarlet, reddish and purple hues, as is apparent from the words of the *Zohar*. But in this realm there is no color whatsoever. All is white.

While on the subject of the eye, we shall explain its content. We have said that the organ is made of the particular *Sefirot* "Wisdom" and "Intelligence" of "Wisdom", and the sense of seeing therein is made of the *Yud* of the *Havaya* which was concealed within and issued there. The extension of all ten *Sefirot* is intimated in the eyes, for the emendation of all the ten *Sefirot* lies in their being arranged as pillars, namely: right, left and center, corresponding to the pillars of "Mercy", "Judgment" and "Compassion". Thus we find that three *Sefirot* head the pillars, from which all the other *Sefirot* spring. "Wisdom" is the head of the right pillar, "Intelligence" is the head of the left pillar, and "Knowledge" is the head of the central pillar. Note that there are three colors in the eyes, and these indicate the three heads of the pillars of the *Sefirot* located there. "Kingdom", the last of the *Sefirot*, is indicated by the pupil of the eye.

We have already explained that two emendations were made in the head of *Atik* by means of "Triumph" and "Glory": these are "the pure wool" and "the opening of the eyes". Still another emendation was performed in the head of *Arik*, and these are the two ears.

They are wrought from the two testicles, but this emendation is not mentioned because these two testicles, being the interior essence of "Triumph" and "Glory", are very much concealed. It is that same essence which is bound with "Foundation". And, since the two ears are exceedingly concealed, we do not mention their emendation.

The last, the seventh emendation of the head is: 7) THE NOSE. This is made of "Kingdom" of *Atik* and just as "Kingdom" is divided into two parts—into "Leah" and "Rachel"—so are there in the nose two openings (nostrils) called *Nukba' de-Pareda sheka'*—the feminine counterpart of the symbolic "window". The symbolic importance of "Leah and Rachel" will be explained in a later chapter.

Chapter
Twelve

We shall now explain in detail the matter of the thirteen emendations of the beard. It has already been noted that those thirteen emendations of the beard were made of the three *Havayas* and the one that comprises them, all of which are found in the "Concealed Wisdom".

In the *Idra* it is stated that the entire beard springs from the brain of the head, and that this beard is divided into thirteen emendations. It begins at the sideburns of the head, and encircles the face and the mouth on both sides, reaching to the navel. On this point the *Idra* says: "This most trusty beard comes forth from the ear and rests around the holy mouth . . . and covers down to the 'navel of the heard.'"

The Supreme Creator designed these thirteen channels for the purpose of bestowing bounty through them to the nether worlds. Thus they are designated as thirteen founts, and because they are made of "Concealed Wisdom", they are further designated as "the thirteen founts from which an abundance of 'good oil' flows". For it is known that "Concealed Wisdom" is symbolized by the term "the good oil". It spreads over the face, and there effects thirteen emendations, of which the details are as follows:

The Thirteen Emendations of the Beard

1. The narrow part of the beard, i.e. the two side-burns of the beard. This is the place below the ears.

2. The upper lip, crossing from one side of the mouth to the other.

3. The break in the center of the lip. It is that break at the center of the lip under the two openings of the nose where no hair appears.

4. The lower lip, where it crosses from one side to the other, as in the case of the upper lip.

5. The break which exists here in the center of this lower lip as it does in the upper lip, and where there is likewise no hair.

6. The place where the beard broadens, beneath the cheeks, close to the mouth.

7. The place of the cheeks themselves, where there is no hair, and which has the appearance of two apples.

8. The upper surface—it is the long hair of the beard which reaches to the navel and is called "mazela" (the fountain of bestowal). This term is derived from a phrase in the Scriptures: "He shall pour the water out of his buckets'.' (Numbers XXIV, 7) Because the bounty of this emendation flows downward.

9. The small hairs which lie between the upper surface, i.e. the place of the 8th emendation, and the subspace which is the 13th emendation.

10. The hair which lies underneath, at the throat.

11.   Thé hair of the beard which ends equally, and does not extend beyond itself at all.

12.   The mouth, which is void of hair, for no hair whatsoever covers the mouth.

13.   The area underneath. These are the long hairs of the beard which, like the 8th emendation, reach to the navel; and they too are called "fountain of bestowal" (mazela), because they flow down below. These two founts are the principal ones in the beard and it is from them that bounty is bestowed to the worlds.

These thirteen emendations of the beard are the thirteen attributes (measures) of compassion which our teacher, Moses, mentioned in Exodus 45, verses 6 and 7, as follows:

1) The Lord God
2) merciful
3) gracious
4 & 5) long suffering
6) and abundant in goodness
7) and truth
8) keeping mercy
9) for thousands
10) forgiving iniquity
11) and transgression
12) and sin
13) and clears

The prophet Micah also mentions these thirteen attributes in Chapter 7, verses 18-20:

1) Who is a God like unto Thee

2) that pardons iniquity
3) and passes by the transgression
4) of the remnant of His heritage.
5) He retains not His anger forever
6) because He delights in mercy
7) He will turn again, He will have compassion upon us
8) He will subdue our iniquities
9) And Thou wilt cast all their sins into the depths of the sea
10) Thou wilt give truth to Jacob
11) Mercy to Abraham
12) which Thou hast sworn unto our fathers
13) from the days of old.

The difference between the attributes mentioned by Micah and those mentioned by Moses is that Micah's are the names of the emendations in their place in *Arik*, while those of Moses are the names of the emendations when they evolve downward into Z'O to be enclothed in his beard. At the time of their descent the names of the emendations are changed and they are called "The Lord God, etc. . . . "

To resume the exposition of the thirteen emendations of the beard, for we have not exhausted this subject with what was said above, these thirteen are the selections which were gathered from the Primordial Kings, and were there emended. Although no shattering occurred in the first three *Sefirot*, nevertheless when the selections rose to their places to be emended, they also rose up to the first three *Sefirot*. Therefore it was said of these thirteen emendations of the beard that they issued from the residue of the brain: in other words, they were issued from that which was selected from the Primordial Kings.

It is already known that the selection is made in the brain, that is, in the Thought, as mentioned in the *Zohar*: "They were all selected in the Thought." In addition, because the thirteen emendations of the beard are channels which extend from the brain, they are also called the "sediment of the brain", or residue of the brain. Because they are formed out of the excrescences which were chosen from the Primordial Kings, they are termed "primordial days." That is, they came into being from the selection of the Primordial Kings, as it says in the *Idra*: "These emendations are called primordial days. They are named the "primordial days of the primordial ones'", and are therefore of the essence of Judgment: but they are *divine* Judgments. It is they who subdue the husks.

Thus, these thirteen emendations of the beard are the individual, encircling *Sefirot* of "Crown" and "Wisdom", which were revealed in the countenance. They are ten encircling *Sefirot* of "Crown" and ten of "Wisdom". There should be twenty, but only fourteen were revealed; namely eight from "Wisdom" and six from "Crown", yet, because one of the emendations comprises two of the encircling *Sefirot*, there are only thirteen, and not fourteen.

We do not know any reason for this, but attribute it to the ineffable Wisdom of the Creator, because He knew that this (amount) and no more was required for the purpose of governing the world.

It is a generally established principle, in matters pertaining to the *Sefirot* and to the *Parezufim*, that wherever we find a single *Sefira* or a single *Parezuf* which required the combination of many entities for its construction, we cannot say that there is a paradox, for it is but one thing. Just so many entities were necessary in order to bring out the one particular entity. So it is in the case of the beard. All the entities mentioned were required for its construction. So we find that in order to complete the beard of Z'O, it was necessary that "Foundation" be split and that the four white hairs of *Arik* be present.

Note that of the encircling *Sefirot* of "Crown" and "Wisdom," which are in the beard, the *Sefirot* of "Wisdom" precede. In the first eight emendations there are the eight *Sefirot* of Wisdom, while the remaining ones come from "Crown". The reason that "Wisdom's" *Sefirot* are first (despite the fact that it is more fitting for "Crown", which is the first of the emendations, to precede "Wisdom"), is that the principal essence of the beard is made of "Concealed Wisdom". Thus the *Sefirot* of "Wisdom" precede those of "Crown", and since these *Sefirot* are encircling ones, they proceed from below and move upward—that is, the *Sefirot* of "Wisdom" start from "Kingdom" and terminate at "Intelligence". The *Sefirot* of "Crown" start from "Foundation", and proceed up to "Mercy". A full description follows.

The first emendation is "The Lord God" and also "Who is a God like unto Thee?"; referring to the narrow part of the beard. This emendation corresponds to "Kingdom" of the encircling *Sefirot* of "Wisdom", and it is called "Lord" (in Hebrew *Lamed Alef*, with a numerical value of- 31) because there are thirty-one powerful short hairs here. This Name is found in both sideburns. Thus, there are two of these Names, one on the right side and one on the left. Each in turn is subdivided into three: 1) *'El Shaddai;* 2) *'El Havaya;* 3) *'El Adni,* making a total of six. However, of the two first mentioned Names, only one is revealed, so that we find 'El in all but five Names.

The *Idra* mentions three worlds which exist in this emendation, and they are represented by the three Names, El. The numerical value of the first Name, when it is spelled out, is 1000; the second is 57; the third 96. This is the subdivision that is spoken of in the *Idra.* However, the secret of the matter is as follows. The beard was made from the selections chosen from the Name 52, known as the Primordial Kings; and for that reason it is called the primordial days. It was here that these days began to be selected and to appear as Powers, which subdued the husks, or the dross that is expelled from the Kings. However, what is here revealed is the selection of three different Kings. They are Bela, Jobab and Husham, and they signify respectively: "Knowledge", "Mercies" and "Powers". And what remained of them? Only the very tough husks, called "furnace and inferno". The source of the selection of the first three Kings is here; this is the hidden meaning of the three worlds mentioned above. And it was from these three worlds that the lower degrees evolved. Namely, the posterior part of "Intelligence", Z'O and *Nukba,* the feminine counterpart of Z'O, and others which belong to the worlds of *B'Y'A*—Creation, Formation and Action. That which has been expelled from all these degrees and has not remained with them, is the unadulterated dross which we call the husk.

Through these sources the husks of excrescences that still remain are subdued. This is related to the subject of unity, which shall be discussed shortly.

Note that in the first *EL,* which is *El Shaddai,* the Light of "Concealed Wisdom" shines with greater force than in the other Names, because *El Shaddai* is closer to "Concealed Wisdom" than the others. In "Concealed Wisdom" is a progression of the Name *Elohim* comprised of *He's* whose numerical value is 1000, which the *Idra* calls: "A thousand worlds which are sealed in the ring," for "Concealed Wisdom" is symbolized by a "ring"— since it is the origin of all the worlds.

Both "The Lord God" and "Who is a God like unto Thee?" are one in that they both represent the first emendation of the beard.

The second emendation is "merciful" and also "remitter" or raiser, of sin", or in the original wording, "that pardons iniquity"; and as we have earlier explained, this emendation is the upper lip and its extension on either side thereof. This emendation is Foundation of the encircling *Sefirot* of "Wisdom" and is called "remitter of sin". It points to the hair which is found on this lip and which rises upward. Hence the reference, "raiser of sin".

The third emendation is represented by the phrase "gracious" and also "and passes by the transgression." We have mentioned that this emendation is the break at the center of the upper lip, where there is no hair. This emendation is "Glory" of the encircling *Sefirot* of "Wisdom", and the reason that there is no hair found there, as previously stated, is that hair is Judgment. It restricts the Light, for everything that restricts is Judgment. In order that the Light which shines from the openings of the nose should pass through without any hindrance, there is no hair in the middle of the upper lip which is directly opposite the nose. It is called "and passes by the transgression" to indicate the passing through of the bounty through this break, without veil or hindrance.*

The fourth emendation is "long" and also "of the remnant of His heritage". We have said that this is the lower lip, extending on both sides, like the upper one. This emendation is "Triumph" of the encircling *Sefirot* of "Wisdom".

The fifth emendation is "suffering" and also "He retains not his anger forever". We have indicated that this is the break in the lower lip where there is no hair, and this emendation is "Beauty" of the encircling *Sefirot* of "Wisdom". The reason there is no hair here is the same as in the case of the third emendation; namely, because it is directly beneath the nose, and the Light which shines from the nose must extend without any hindrance. Here too, there is no hair beneath the mouth so that the Light of the mouth is able to extend to the nether beings without any obstruction. The name of the emendation itself indicates this.

------

* Tr. N. The Hebrew for "transgression" is *"pesha"* which transposed, reads "shefa" meaning "bounty"—thus, in spite of the transgression, He transmits the bounty, without veil or hindrance.

The name of the sixth emendation is "and abundant
in goodness" and also "because He delights in mercy".
We have stated earlier that this is the place below the
cheeks where the beard broadens. This emendation is
"Power" of the encircling *Sefirot* of "Wisdom" and it
is called "abundant in goodness" because here "Mercy"
is even more greatly extended than in the others; and
"Mercy" as you will recall, tempers the Judgments.
Understand that *we-rab hesed* ("and abundant in goodness") amounts to 280, which is the number of the final
letters *Mem, Nun, Zaddi Pe, Hof,* (M'N'Z'P'K,) which
are 280 "Powers". They are tempered by the "abundance
in goodness which are the 280 "Mercies".

The seventh emendation is "and Truth" and also
"He will turn again, He will have compassion upon us".
We have said that this emendation corresponds to the
area of the cheeks, where there is no hair and where the
cheeks resemble two apples. This emendation is "Mercy"
of the encircling *Sefirot* of "Wisdom". It is called "He
will turn again, He will have compassion upon us" because there are periods when these two "apples" shine
below and other periods when they do not. As it says in
the *Idra*: "He will return." This signifies times of concealment and times of revelation. Hence, "He will turn
again, He will have compassion upon us."* In these
two "apples" there are 370 Lights, in other words, two
Names *El* (*Alef Lamed* spelled out) amounting to 370.
Of these the *Idra* says: "These apples . . . shine into 370
sides." They are the 370 Lights mentioned above. Of

---

* TR. N. Until He "turns again" to "have compassion",
concealment prevails.

the 370, 150 evolve below to Z'O and the balance of 220 remains with him. *Arik* is here designated by the name of "Erek Apaiym" to indicate the 220 (*Resh Chaf*) Lights. For together with the vessel containing the 220 Lights, we get the number of "*Erek*". This is the seventh emendation in which are comprised the first six emendations, as it is expressed in the *Idra*". "This is the seventh emendation in which contains six . . ." It is called "And truth".

The eighth emendation is "keeping mercy" and also "He will subdue our iniquities". We have already explained that this emendation is the upper surface of the beard, and that it reaches to the navel. This emendation is "Intelligence" of the encircling *Sefirot* of "Wisdom", and also "Foundation" of the encircling *Sefirot* of "Crown", both being united.

In this connection we have said previously that two *Sefirot* unite in one emendation and that there are therefore thirteen and not fourteen emendations. This emendation is called the "upper fountain", because there are two fountains: the upper area and the lower area. Since this is the upper area, it is called "upper fountain" and this *mazela* is masculine. The "lower fountain" (13th emendation) is the feminine polarity, and these unite for the purpose of transmitting bounty to the nether worlds. The precise manner in which bounty is extended will be taken up later.

In this 8th emendation there is one *Havaya* spelled with *Yud's* of which the numerical value is 72, connoting the word *Hesed* (which has the same numerical value). By the Light of this emendation the outer forces (husks) are subdued in such a manner that they cannot draw sustenance from the sacred fount; hence they flee it. This is what the words "He will subdue our iniquities" mean. In other words, by the power of this emendation the sins are subdued, for they are the actual husks and outer forces. As it says in the *Idra*: "and whoever sees this emendation is subdued and vanquished by it," for it is said "He will subdue our iniquities."

The ninth emendation is "for thousands" and also "and Thou wilt cast all their sins into the depths of the sea;" we have said that this emendation are the small hairs which lie between the upper and lower areas. This emendation is "Glory" of the encircling *Sefirot* of "Crown". In this emendation there are three Names AHY'H (comprised of He's) which have the same numerical value as *Adni* and *Elohim*. All begin with the letter Alef and connote the expression "for thousands" (lo—alofim).*

These are the Names to which the husks have access for nourishment, for they are of the feminine polarity. When the divine Power wishes to eliminate all nourishing of these evil spirits, the fount of "keeping mercy"— (which is complete "Mercy" since Mercy of the inner *Sefirot* of "Crown" is located there) shines into this emendation so that the husks cannot draw nourishment from his Light. This emendation is the sacred Power and as it is expressed in the *Idra*: "and from this place all who seek to accuse man are reprimanded and subdued." For this reason this emendation is termed "depths of the sea" (*mezulot*), because it subdues the husks which are

---

* TN. N. *alef* means "a thousand."

called "the deep darkness" (zalmowet). The letters of *Mezulot* are the same as those of *zalmowet*. (interchangeable).

The tenth emendation is "forgiving iniquity" and also "Thou wilt give truth to Jacob." As we have said, this emendation is the hair which is at the throat. This emendation is "Triumph" of the encircling *Sefirot* of "Crown", and since it is from this *Sefira,* it is called "Glory" because the *Sefira* of "Triumph", as we learn elsewhere, is called "Glory". The *Idra* describes this emendation in the words of the Bible "and from the Glory of His Majesty", saying "Those hairs which are underneath the beard are called 'Glory of His Majesty.' "

The eleventh emendation is "and transgression" as well as "Mercy to Abraham" and we have said that this emendation refers to the hairs of the beard which are all even and do not protrude at all beyond each other. This emendation is "Beauty" of the encircling *Sefirot* of "Crown".

The twelfth emendation is "and seen" and also "which Thou hast sworn unto our ancestors." We have said that this emendation is the mouth, which is free from hair, for no hair at all covers it. This emendation is "Judgment" of the encircling *Sefirot* of "Crown". The reason there is no hair found here is so that the mouth remain free and the bounty be extended without hindrance. Again, as it is stated in the *Idra*: "Therefore no hair is found upon the sacred mouth because of the Spirit which issues therefrom, and no foreign element is able to mingle with or even approach it." From this mouth issues a Spirit which is subdivided into 37 paths, indicating *Hebel ha-peh* the "breath of the mouth."

Hebel has the numerical value of 37, which is the amount of the spelled-out letters of the Name 63, YHW'H if we take the spelled-out letters minus the initials of the letters.*   Of this it is said in the Idra: "When that Spirit issues forth it is divided into 37,000 sides, and it is the very Spirit which the prophets were enveloped."   It is called the "mouth of God" and was the Spirit which cloaked the holy ancestors.   Therefore this emendation is called: "which Thou hast sworn unto our ancestors."

The thirteenth emendation is "and clears" and also "from the days of old."   We have already explained that this emendation is the lower area of the beard and that it is extended to the navel, just like the surface area. This emendation is "Mercy" of the encircling *Sefirot* of "Crown" and is called the "lower fount" since it is the lower area of the beard.   It is the feminine polarity in relation to all the other emendations, and comprises all the earlier ones.   "This thirteenth one comprises all," says the *Idra*.

As stated previously, the thirteenth emendations of the beard were made of the three *Havayas*, plus an additional one that forms them—both of which are present in "Concealed Wisdom".   Thus they are thirteen, namely: the twelve letters of the three *Havayas*, and the thirteenth, which embraces them.   The first twelve emendations were made of the twelve letters in the three *Havayas*, and the thirteenth emendation, the last, is made

---

    * TR. N.   Thus *Waw-Dalet* of the spelled-out *Yud* amounts to 10; *Yud* of the spelled-out *He'* is also 10; *Alef-Waw* of the *Waw* makes 7; and *Yud* of the final *He'* is again 10; the sum total being 37.

of that which comprises the twelve. Since it is made from this essence, this last emendation also embraces the thirteen emendations. Because it comprises the whole beard it is called "from the days of old," for the "beard" itself is similarly defined.

In this emendation is found the Name AHY'H formed with *Yud's* and having a numerical value of 161, the number of *we-nakeh* ("and clears"). When these two founts unite (the thirteenth and the eight) then power is given to the fount known as "and clears", for the purpose of "clearing" or purifying, and extracting all the Sparks that fell into the husks. The name "and clears" also points to this.

Whenever the Supreme Emanator will desire to return the world to the perfection it had at the beginning of creation—that is, to withdraw all the sacred Sparks from the oppressors who have seized them—then this beard will bestir itself for it is "she" that subdues the husks. For *she* is of the essence of power, and she will bestir herself through the power of this fount (*mazela*) called "and clears" to clear everything tyranized by the husks—both what was left there as dross from the Primordial Kings, and the Sparks which they have snatched from the Divine Spirit.

This fount will perform yet another action. That is, when the husks see that all their sustenance is vanishing from them they will want to rise after the Sparks in order to receive from them some kind of bounty. But by the power of this fount they will be subdued, and will be unable to rise. Then the husks will remain lifeless. The Divine Power will bestir itself and It alone will remain, pure and without any admixture whatsoever. In the words of Isaiah: "And the Lord alone shall be exalted in that day." (Isaiah II, 11).

Just as the Divine Spirit will be cleared of dross, so will Israel below become distinct and segregated from the nations of the world, for the Israelites are the branches of the Divine Spirit and the barbarians among the nations are the branches of the husks; and the power of the branch is drawn in the same direction as its Source. In this way, Israel will be separated from the barbarians; as the Divine Spirit will be divorced completely from the husks. Then the world will remain completely perfected as never before. Israel will be redeemed. The redemption will be so complete that there will never again be exile, for it is already known that the single purpose of all the periods of exile was to select the Sparks of the Holy Spirit from amidst the husks. Since at that time, through the power of the fount entitled "and clears", the entire selection will have been made to the extent that nothing will be left in the husks not even an infinitesimal trace. No exile will any longer be necessary for the purpose of selecting Sparks, since they will already have been extracted. The words of the prophets will be fulfilled: "He will destroy death for ever; and the Lord God will wipe away tears from off all faces; and the rebuke of his people shall He take away from off all the earth; for the Lord hath spoken it." (Isaiah XXV, 8)

And th Lord shall be King over all the earth; in that day shall the Lord be One and His Name one." (Zechariah XIV, 9)

Chapter
Thirteen

Up to this point we have explained the particulars regarding the thirteen emendations of the beard. Now we come to the explanation of the distribution of the bounty by way of the two founts to the lower *Parezufim* (Heavenly Persons). This description comes from the writings of Rabbi Hayyim Vital.

First, the matter of bestowal, the most significant aspect of all this great wisdom. Remember that a number of luminaries are found in the Divine Spirit, each having its own specific function. There are, to begin with, luminaries that stand prepared to draw bounty through their channels, and others to work emendations, as though to provide the "spices" for the "food". In order to understand this concept thoroughly, let us compare the channels to a water faucet. For like the water in the faucet, bestowal must come precisely measured, neither too much, nor too little at a time. The heavenly channels are opened up to a degree that befits each particular bestowal. Let us examine the terms "opening" and "closing".

All the operations of the heavenly supervision depend on the intermingling of the three Lights: "Mercy", "Judgment" and "Compassion". Judgment seals or closes, and Mercy amply bestows. Therefore when

"Judgment" exerts its power to a great degree the Light is restricted, but when he weakens and "Mercy" exerts its power, then bounty is increased. But there are degrees and measures in their respective exertions of power— just as there are degrees and varying measures in the water faucet. That accounts for the varying measures of bestowal granted on weekdays, on Sabbaths, and on holidays.

When "Mercy" exerts its power, the bestowal increases. When it weakens, the bestowal decreases. However, many things are required in order to establish the bestowal in its different measures. Tempering is required for "Judgment", garments are required for "Mercy": might is required for Light to strengthen itself in its descent; and protection for the Light, so as to preserve it from the husks is required as well. That is why what we have called luminaries are present, in addition to the channels of bestowal. All serve to run the system correctly. Indeed, there are many luminaries, but we do not know them all. For the Emanator, blessed be He, made them, and He knows their paths, even if we do not.

Now to go on to the channels of bestowal themselves, for they are chief factors in the drawing of the bounty needed for the world. From the Source down to the *Parezuf Atik* everything is in a state of great concealment: but from *Atik* down, more is revealed, with the bounty beginning to be unveiled in *Atik's Arik* receptor.

The matter of "union" of the Lights represents one of the most arcane aspects of the creation. Because the Emanator arranged the attributes in the order of right and left—"Mercy" and "Judgment"— bounty must

likewise descend in this manner. Therefore it must pass
from "Mercy" to "Judgment", taking energy from both
in order for it to be complete and appropriate for giving
sustenance to all beings. Nevertheless, there is bounty
which inclines more to the right, namely to "Mercy";
and a bounty which inclines to "Judgment". These
represent alternately, the masculine and feminine pre-
ponderances. In the words of the Talmud: ". . . the
lower of which triumphs." Yet, the supervision of the
two goes forth with common consent and the bounty
emerges whole, as it must be.

Only the Emanator Blessed be He Himself can
grant this bounty to the worlds below; no created being
can ever claim this power. The bounty is uniform
(immutable) because the Sefirot approach Him from
below and upwards and because their arousal is always
the same quantitatively, though not qualitatively. So
that when the first Sefirot is aroused, all the others follow
suit, reaching all the way to the Emanator. He bestows
the essence of bounty to them, Empowering them to act.
In this manner, every recipient receives equally.

The channels of bestowal are themselves actually the
vessels that go through the process of uniting. One can
trace the descent of the bestowal as it passes through the
attributes, from one Sefira to another.

"Mercy" and "Judgment" of Atik are enclosed in
"Crown" and "Wisdom" of Arik. This "Crown" and
"Wisdom" are as male and female. "Crown" is male, head
of the entire right pillar, (also male), and is built from
the Name 45. "Concealed Wisdom" is head of the entire

left pillar, which is female, and is built from the Name
52.

"Foundation" is the same for both pillars since
"Foundation" here is used by the male, and the "Diadem"
('*Atarah*) is used by the female. It is there that the
union of *Arik* and its feminine polarity takes place.
However, there will be no mention about the drawing
of bounty as a result of this union. For actually this
union is not located where the nether beings can receive
from it—especially Father and Mother—since these two
are above it. The secret here is a profound one, for
union merely consists of the mutual consent of the attributes. We find that there is a type of union known as
"kissing", and another in which the "Foundations" of
different worlds unite. They indicate that there is unity
and agreement ,between the attributes from beginning to
end. This is a profound and difficult path in the wisdom,
requiring much reflection on the part of the student for
the term "union" in this context means *perfect agreement.*

The beard, as you already know, issues from "Concealed Wisdom", and Father and Mother stand beneath
the beard. Thus *MYAN DUCHRIN* and *MYAN
NUKVIN* are drawn into "Crown" and "Wisdom" from
"Mercy" and "Judgment" (of *Atik*), then they are extended from the very beginning to the end of *Arik* in
order to effect such a union of absolute agreement. Subsequently, the completed bounty returns and issues into
the beard from "Concealed Wisdom". There, in the
beard itself, the bounty is drawn by way of the two
founts, the fount of "keeping mercy" and that of

"clears". All the other emendations are represented by the Lights which emend the bounty, while the two founts known as "keeping mercy" and "clears" are the ones that draw it out.

Note that the bounty is drawn by way of the fount "and clears" to its end, which reaches the navel. There at the end, Z'O (Zeir Anpin) is nourished. But Father and Mother, who stand beneath the fount, are, according to Rabbi Shimon ben Yohai, also included in it. Therefore, Father and Mother take the bounty at its source, as it extends into the fount: This is considered to be the principal bounty which sustains, for that which Z'O receives is only reflected glow. When this principal bounty enters into "and clears", it enters first into the brain of Father and Mother. It must go through their "Crown" which is also the throat of *Arik*. Then it returns to the back and enters the interior, issuing from the palate to the throat. This is in accord with the sequential order, whereby the throat, ("Intelligence") is to receive from the palate ("Wisdom"), and thereafter to enter through the throat into Father and Mother.

After the entrance of Father and Mother into ZO'N, the bounty is granted to the latter, which is consequently emended through the union of Father and Mother. The bounty, further perfected by this union, is thereafter issued into the worlds as far down as the world of Action. Here, all beings receive their nourishment for sustenance from it.

Anyone who can grasp this matter of God's bounty will apprehend His greatness, for it is by means of great and majestic wisdom that the bounty issues forth, and is apportioned to the angels, His servants, and to all the other created beings.

We have previously stated that "Knowledge" of *Arik*—which, unlike the other *Parzufim* that reside in the head, "resides between the shoulders of Adam Kadmon. In order to thoroughly understand this matter, it is necessary to know what this "Knowledge" is, and from what it is made. For the *Sefirot* are only ten, as it says in the *Book of Creation* (*Sefer Yezira*)—"ten and not eleven"—and when we count this "Knowledge" (*D'aath*) into the total of the *Sefirot*, then there are eleven. How can this be?

First let us examine "Knowledge" of Z'O, and from this all the other *Parezufim* will be understood. It must be borne in mind that the Supreme Emanator issued ten *Sefirot* for the purpose of governing the world, but that the chief functions of administration rest with the seven lower *Sefirot*. The first three *Sefirot* serve only as radiance and as additional Light with which to amend the seven lower *Sefirot*, innovating those below with enough new Light for governing the world.

This principle applies equally to the world of Emanation in general as well as to the *Parezuf* of Z'O. For all men's actions depend upon the seven *Sefirot* of Emanation that reside in the collective *Parezufim* of that world.

Arik and Father and Mother, which are above them, serve only to emend the seven lower *Sefirot* .for the purpose of governing the world. Likewise, in the *Parezuf* of Z'O, *his* seven lower *Sefirot* (and principal elements) govern the world, while his first three *Sefirot*, serve only as a supplement, for the revelation of new Light whereby to innovate the world. All the *Sefirot* are made for the purpose of governing the world, but the principal functions of government are performed by the seven lower ones whereas the first three emanate and infuse them with power.

"Crown", "Wisdom" and "Intelligence", which are the first three *Parezufim*, are designed to emend Z'O and the feminine polarity for the governing of the world; it is by virtue of these illuminations that ZO'N own first three *Sefirot* ("Crown", "Wisdom" and "Intelligence") are made. "Crown" is made for Z'O from the illumination of *Arik*, while "Wisdom" and "Intelligence" are made from the illumination of Father and Mother. These *Sefirot* comprise the brains of this *Parezuf* (And the brains are considered to be merely supplemental.)

When the two brains have been formed in Z'O he acquires a third one called "Knowledge" (Da'at), a composite of both five "Mercies" derived from "Wisdom" and five "Powers" "Intelligence". The "Mercies" exist for the purpose of emending the *Parezuf* of Z'O itself, and the "Powers" are meant to perfect his feminine counterpart. The relationship between "Mercies" and "Powers" is analogous to the relationship of male to female.

"Knowledge" of Z'O is comprised of "Powers", despite the fact that they are not intended as part of his Emendation but rather for that of the feminine counterpart. That is because Z'O and *Nukba* are termed "one person". This interdependence prevails even when she becomes separated from him and constitutes an

individual *Parezuf;* she nonetheless remains as one half
of Z'O. This relationship demands that all her emendations pass through Z'O to be considered complete. Thus
Z'O comprises both the five "Mercies" and five "Powers".

The first three *Sefirot* come to Z'O from *Arik* and
Father and Mother. They shine upon him, thereby
engendering in him the three first *Sefirot.* These three
Sefirot ("Crown", "Wisdom" and "Intelligence") form
his upper *Parezufim,* yet "knowledge" represents Z'O
himself, specifically in the form of the six *Sefirot* that
take root in him when he is bestowed with "Crown",
"Wisdom", and "Intelligence"—or, the brain. The brain
(now referred to as "Knowledge") is born after the entry
of the first three *Sefirot.* For, after Z'O is amended
by the power of his newly revealed illumination, the
six lower *Sefirot* are also considered to be emended, and
in this way the third brain, called "Knowledge" comes
into being. In other words, the six *Sefirot* of Z'O
are now crowned and emended by the inner Light.
In fact, Z'O has never really lacked these six *Sefirot*
(even before the formulation of the brain), but it is the
power of the newly revealed Light—itself no less than
the very essence of these six *Sefirot*—which projects
the brain into existence.

This brain is considered to be the soul of the six
Sefirot, for it spreads throughout the body of Z'O in
order to emend the degrees, much like the soul within
the human body. "Mercies", which constitute the principal extension of this brain into the body of Z'O,
occupy only the five *Sefirot*: "Mercy", "Judgment",
"Beauty", "Triumph" and "Glory"; immediately fol-

lowing this extension the five *Sefirot* form an aggregate in "Foundation", as well as in "Kingdom". Z'O contains no more than the extension of these five *Sefirot*. Hence, the initial extension of "Knowledge" takes place in the five *Sefirot*. Moreover, the "Mercies" are doubled, rising also to the first three *Sefirot*, so that all of Z'O's ten *Sefirot* are emended by this inner Light. Nevertheless, it is the five *Sefirot* that are most important. In the same manner the "Judgments" are issued into the body of the feminine counterpart in order to emend *her Parezuf* with inner Light.

Because this brain ("Knowledge") is the inner Light of the six *Sefirot*, it has no vessel. It is all inner Light. An apparent paradox arises, however, when we learn that during the extension of the brain into Z'O, the vessels of "Mercy", "Judgment" and "Beauty" become "Wisdom", "Intelligence" and "Knowledge". "Beauty" therefore forms a vessel for Knowledge. The explanation of this paradox entails the hidden reason for the alternation between "Knowledge" and "Crown", and runs as follows.

Neither "Crown" nor "Knowledge" can be counted as part of the other ten *Sefirot*; for, as we have already learned, "Crown", is that which encircles the *Parezuf* without forming a part of it, and "Knowledge" lacks a vessel and is the pure inner Light. All the other *Sefirot* possess both body and soul—i.e. outer and inner substance. Since this is the case, we might be led to conclude that the number of *Sefirot* is nine and not ten. However, the truth of the matter is that the vessel belonging to "Beauty" rises to the place of

"Knowledge" without enclosing it, and merges instead with the vessel that forms the lower part of "Crown" (the cranium) to encompass "Knowledge". At this juncture the inner "Knowledge", and the vessel of "Beauty" which rose to meet it (and is now therefore an actual part of "Crown's" vessel) become one *Sefira*, thus forming the tenth *Sefira*.

At times, emphasizing its role as inner substance, we call this *Sefira* "Knowledge"; but when we refer to its role as a vessel, we call it "Crown". In this way, it comprises both. This means that, although we count "Crown" among the ten *Sefirot*, we do not refer to the *actual* "Crown", since it is not really part of the *Parezuf* in question. That is why it is called *Keter*, from the term *keteris*, or that which "encompasses". What we are actually referring to is the vessel belonging to "Beauty", which rises upward, joins with the vessel belonging to "Crown" and thereby assumes its title. Together, these two encompass the brain, while "Beauty" serves as a vessel for "Knowledge".

The brain of "Knowledge' emends the six *Sefirot* that comprise Z'O. It functions as their inner Light, or, in other words, is their brain. The entire process takes place at the time of the general emendation. During the period of the "Primordial Kings" however, "Knowledge"—encompassed by the uppermost third of "Beauty"—was situated between the shoulders of Z'O. What then became of the Light of "Beauty" that radiated in the remaining two-thirds of the vessel? Immediately after the extension, these two-thirds were sufficiently augmented to encloth the entire *Sefira*. Now that "Knowledge" formed part of the "Crowns", * it became closely united with "Mercy" and "Power", the three comprising one interdependent unit. Bela corresponds to "Knowledge", Jobab to "Mercy", and Husham to "Power".

When this particular "Knowledge" was shattered, only the parts that belonged to it broke. But the parts belonging to "Beauty" remained there, and were not shattered until later when "Beauty" itself was shattered.

Everything regarding the *Sefira* "Knowledge" in the *Parezuf* Z'O applies equally to Father and Mother. For their "Knowledge" also serves the purpose of emending their seven lower *Sefirot* with inner Light, or brain. Every *Parezuf* is an aggregate of all five *Parezufim,* and the seven lower *Sefirot* of Father and Mother are just the same as ZO'N of the collective world of Emanation; hence their "Knowledge" is exactly the same as "Knowledge" of Z'O, for in both *Parezufim* it resides in the head, close to the brain. Whereas in *Arik,* "Knowledge" is situated between the shoulders. Note that the complete emendation of all *Parezufim* is dependent on "Knowledge'.

We find then that the "Mercies" serve to emend the masculine principle and that the "Powers" serve to emend the feminine principle. Since here *Arik* and its feminine counterpart, the two great luminaries, are equal (one being on the right and one on the left) the

---

* TR. N.   Referred to here in the plural because it constitutes "Crown", as well as the upper third of "Beauty", which is thus also considered as a "Crown".

"Mercies" and "Powers" issue from "Foundation" of the feminine counterpart of *Atik,* which is situated in the chest of the collective *Parezuf.* Then, the five Mercies" spread out in his body, but rather return, rising above the "Foundation" and half are revealed at the base of "Foundation" on downward. The "Powers" are extended to the left side, and all five of them are unveiled.

Now to examine the order of their extension and issuance from "Foundation" of *Atik.* It is known that the Names of 45 and 52, of which the *Parezuf Atik* was made, were completely united so that one formed the posterior part and one of the anterior—although that particular *Parezuf* is considered to be all "face" This "Foundation" of *Atik,* which is placed opposite "Knowledge" of *Arik,* is therefore made of the two components, namely, male and female belonging to the "Foundation" of *Atik,* which are united as one.

However, the "Mercies" and "Powers" were unable to stand together as one within "Foundation" (*Yesod*) of *Atik,* for this "Foundation" is the male polarity and is therefore narrower than the "Foundation" of the female polarity. Because of its form, the male polarity could only contain one of the two, either the "Mercies" or the "Powers", and so prevented them from uniting in "Foundation" of the female polarity as well.

The "Powers" are extended first to "Foundation", for they are the lowest order of the brain; this matter of precedence causes the "Mercies", which come later, to remain above the "Powers". Later, when the "Mercies" come to "Foundation", they expel these "Powers" which are then issued by way of the mouth of "Founda-

tion" into the body of *Arik*. However, they do not
spread to the right side. Half are veiled in the vessel
and encircling "Foundation" on the outside—half of
them on the right and half on the left. This happens
because the "Powers", in relation to the "Mercies", are
as feminine to masculine, and since their great desire
is to unite with the "Mercies", they rise and encircle
them out-side of "Foundation". In this way, the
"Mercies" and the "Powers" stand together from the
chest on upwards—"Mercies" on the inside, "Powers"
on the outside.

Subsquently, when the "Mercies" issue from Foundation", and find half of the "Powers" on the right side,
they thrust them over to the left. It is necessary to
know that from over to the left. It is necessary to
issue is under the chest—for the concealed ones are to
tion". Although the place from which the 2½ "Mercies"
issue is under the chest—for the concealed ones are to
be found above — nevertheless, when they emerge,
they immediately rise above the chest and thrust over
to the left the "Powers" which they find there. After-
wards, they spread themselves below the temper and
modify the "Powers" which are opposite them.

The "Powers" that were on the right side then move
to the left, above the chest, where they find their remaining half. Since there is no room above the chest
for all five "Powers", those that, to begin with, were
on the right side, and were therefore superior, now
remain above the chest on the left side, pushing those
that were originally there down below the chest. This
locates half of the "Mercies" within "Foundation",

"above the chest, and half of them below, outside Foundation"; while all the "Powers" are outside, half of them above and half below.

These four divisions of Lights are found in the body of *Arik* and for this reason there are four *Parezurim* clothing *Arik* from the throat to the navel:

1) Father
2) Mother
3) Israel the Ancient
4) Understanding

From the illumination of the "Mercies" which are concealed in "Foundation" comes Father, and in this connection the *Zoher says*: "Father" is hidden and concealed," having been drawn from these covered and concealed "Mercies". From the unveiled "Mercies", Israel the Ancient is drawn. From the "Powers" which are above the chest, Mother is drawn, and from those below the chest, Understanding is drawn.

Since the difference between the "Mercies" and the "Powers", is that the "Powers" are *all* extended and revealed while only half of the "Mercies" are revealed and the other half are covered, it influences the nature of the *Parezufim*. Thus Father, and Israel the Ancient are two distinct and separate *Parezufim*. Simply because the "Mercies" tended are disunited: while Mother, and Understanding, which are drawn from the "Powers" (which are coequal in their extension), are united with each other, for the feet of Mother are located in the head of Understanding.

There are two kinds of "Mercies" and "Powers". The first kind are those which came at the beginning, served to amend the *Parezuf*, and were then extended in the manner above described; but the second type are perpetually involved in bestowing to the worlds. When these second types appear, they illuminate the first as well. Because of the partition of "Foundation" which separates them, the "Powers" that are situated above "Foundation", and the illumination of the concealed "Mercies", from which Father issued, indirectly receive energy from the "Mercies" and "Powers" extending there. The "Mercies" and "Powers" situated below the "Foundation", however, receive direct illumination; because of this difference, since each of their Lights is divided into two rays, these latter ones possess sufficient power to issue four branches, or two *Parezufim*. (This will be described shortly.) However, when the second type of "Mercies" and "Powers" extend they do not expel the "Mercies" that remain in "Foundation", as these are already considered part of the body of "Foundation" itself, and serve as a transmitter for the new bounty of "Powers" and "Mercies"—in as much as the Light is drawn because of the awakening of these lower ones. These channels permit "Mercies" and "Powers" to extend and pass through.

Until now we have been discussing the *Parezuf* of *Arik*, in all its particulars. Now let us turn to the details pertaining to the *Parezufim* of Father and Mother, which clothe *Arik* from the throat to the navel.

First recall that Father and Mother are synonymous with "Wisdom" and "Intelligence" of the collective world of Emanation. But, like all the *Parezufim*, each of these encompasses ten *Sefirot*. We have already mentioned earlier that the *Parezufim* of Father and Mother are separated from each other, in such a way that each individually comprises the two Names 45 and 52. This is not the case with the *Parezufim* of *Atik* and *Arik* and their feminine counterparts, for those are united so that the Name 45 is considered to be male and the Name 52 female.

Father is composed of half of "Intelligence" of the Name 45 and of the seven lower *Sefirot* of "Wisdom" belonging to the Name 52—the first three *Sefirot* having been appropriated by *Atik* as his feminine counterpart. Mother is composed of the lower half of "Intelligence" of 45 and the six lower *Sefirot* of "Intelligence" of 52, since the first four *Sefirot* were taken by *Atik* as his feminine counterpart.

These two *Parezufim* are subdivided into four, because of the different types of illumination coming to them from the "Mercies" and "Powers" of *Arik*. Collectively, these *Parezufim*, from the chest up, are called "Father and Mother": and from that point downwards, they are called "Israel the Ancient" and "Understanding". We find then that the upper Father and Mother enclothe *Arik* down to the chest, one on his right and one on his left, while from the chest down to the navel, *Arik* is clothed by Israel the Ancient, and Understanding, also divided between right and left.

Israel the Ancient, and Understanding clothe the upper Father and Mother from their mutual chest downward. Bear in mind that the inclusive Father and Mother are called Father and Mother only as far as the chest, because up to that point they are bare and unclothed.

From the chest down, however, they are enclothed by Israel the Ancient, and by Understanding, so that we no longer consider that portion of them as part of their *Parezufim*. Instead, from this point on they are represented respectively by Israel the Ancient, and by Understanding.

This explains why in one place the *Parezufim* of the upper Father and Mother are clothed by the *Parezufim* of Israel the Ancient, and Understanding from their chest down—so that these four end evenly inside—and why elsewhere the feet of Mother ("Intelligence") are in the head of Understanding so that the upper Father and Mother end in the chest at the place where Israel the Ancient, and Understanding begin.

The nature of the upper Lights is such that they change according to their position, and that is what is meant when we say that the feet of "Intelligence" are in the head of Understanding. This situation obtains only between Mother and Understanding, and not in the case of Father and Israel the Ancient.

Nevertheless, both Father and Mother end evenly at the chest, because her soles, which are located on the *inside,* are not considered as part of her, and that which is seen outside is an equal terminus. Also, when we say that upper Father and Mother reach to the chest of *Arik,* and that Israel the Ancient, and Understanding reach to the navel, we refer to that which is seen of these *Parezufim*. Whereas on the inside, all four clothe *Arik* down to the navel and end equally. This is an important fact.

The upper Father and Mother are composed of the Names 45 and 52 of Father, while Israel the Ancient,

and Understanding are composed of the Names 45 and
52 of Mother. When Mother and Father united, Father
gave his Name 52 to Mother in exchange for her Name
45, which he thereupon gave to Israel the Ancient.
Mother gave her Name 52 to Understanding. Thus the
Name 45 belonging to Father and the 45 belonging to
Mother are both in the right side: Father has one Name
45 and Israel the Ancient has the other; similarly, the
Name 52 of both are on the left side. Mother has one
and Understanding the other. The uniting of the upper
Father with Mother, as well as that of Israel the Ancient
with Understanding therefore corresponds to the uniting
of the Names 45 and 52.

Father and Mother commence from the throat of
Arik. Their "Crowns" clothe his throat, one on the
right, the other on the left; their remaining *Sefirot*
clothe his body—Father the right arm, that is, his
"Mercy", and Mother the left arm, his "Power". In this
connection, the *Zohar says*: "Father is united with Mercy
and Mother with Power, because they clothe Mercy and
Power respectively."

The "Wisdom", "Intelligence" and "Knowledge"
belonging to Father and Mother were formed from the
arms of *Arik,* and from his body came the rest of their
Sefirot. The glow of his (Arik's) *Sefirot* alternates in
the making of Father and Mother: their "Wisdom" "Intelligence" and "Knowledge" come from his first sections
of "Mercy", "Power" and "Beauty", their "Mercy",
"Power", and "Beauty" were formed out of the second
sections of "Mercy", "Power" and "Beauty" belonging
to *Arik;* and from the third section of "Mercy", "Power"

and "Beauty" of *Arik,* came their "Triumph", "Glory" and "Foundation". Thereafter, these *Sefirot* all rose and enveloped *Arik* in the preceding order.

It is necessary to know that the union of Father and Mother is perpetual, that it never ceases, and that these *Parezufim* are not dependent upon the actions of man. Therefore, the *Zohar* speaks of them as "Friends who never part." Two kinds of union exist between Father and Mother: "outer", a union between the outer Lights, and "inner", a union of the inner Lights. The former which takes place only in the upper Father and Mother—never ceases. It requires no arousal whatsoever from below. But the union of the inner Lights, namely that union of Father and Mother which is performed for the purpose of bringing brain to Z'O, is not perpetual, but rather intermittent. Here, the arousal by the lower beings (men) is necessary in order to bring it about. All four *Parezufim*: Father and Mother, Israel the Ancient, and Understanding, are included in this union—the four becoming but two.

Bear in mind that between Father and Mother there is an intermediary—"Knowledge"—which unites them. This is represented by the fountain of "and clears" (*mazel wenakeh*) of the beard.

It is important to note that the *Parezufim* of Israel the Ancient, and Understanding, from their chest downward, are divided in two. These are called the second Israel the Ancient, and the second Understanding, and it is the *Sefirot* "Triumph", "Glory" and "Foundation" of these two which are drawn into Z'O as the latter's brain. These three *Sefirot* are called the third Israel the Ancient, and the third Understanding.

Remember that at times the *Parezufim* of the upper Father and Mother, Israel the Ancient, and Understanding are united as one, and that what was previously "Foundation" of upper Father and Mother becomes the location for the chest of the collective *Parezuf*. However, this occurs only at the time of union. There are other occasions when Israel the Ancient, and Understanding rise and are included in Father and Mother in order to unite; and yet other times when the upper Father and Mother descend and are included in Israel the Ancient, and Understanding.

The first pregnancy, which occurs in order to engender the six *Sefirot* (Z'O), sees Israel the Ancient, and Understanding rise into upper Father and Mother. In the second pregnancy, which takes place so that the first three *Sefirot* may be supplemented to Z'O, upper Father and Mother descend into both Israel the Ancient, and Understanding. These periodic changes in the *Parezufim* occur during the first and second maturity of Z'O.

This procedure will be further enumerated during discussions regarding Z'O and his acquisition of brain.

PART II

Chapter One

The Sefirot

The *Sefirot* are the Creator's attributes. He devised these measures or vessels for Himself in order to fulfill the needs of His created beings. These measures are not on a par with the Creator's own perfection and true completeness of being, but are rather limits invented by His will and desire, in accordance with the requirements of the beings He desired to create. They comprise all the attributes that are related to Him by reason of His acts, in other words, all that may be discerned in His acts, for example: dominion, compassion, anger, justice, graciousness, knowledge, and numerous other traits characterizing His acts. However, we must differentiate between these attributes as inherent in the soul of man, and the so-called characteristics of the Creator, blessed be He, to whom the term "character" is inapplicable in the first place.

Indeed, these "Attributes" of the Creator are nothing but a means of supervision or administration which He employs in the form of Lights that emit energy to His created beings. For example, when we refer to the "Mercy" of the Creator, we are not referring to a characteristic trait in Him, but rather to a single type of illumination which He sends forth from Himself. It is more in the nature of a specific act executed by Him. The same is true of other "attributes", like anger, graciousness, the knowledge of things, and all other ways in which we may depict His acts. These are all really types of radiations which He emits into the paths decreed and devised by Himself for His created beings. The *Sefirot* are therefore integral to Him, and manifest His Mercy, His Graciousness, His Justice, His Righteousness, and so on. However, His Mercy, Graciousness and Justice are not traits of character in Him as are the characteristics in a human soul; they are more like the Lights in a theater that are being emitted and supervised by a director who is in complete control yet is outside of them. To one ray we apply the term "Mercy"; to another "Judgment", to still another "Compassion", and so on down the line covering all the particular radiations.

The chief function of the *Sefirot* is the extension of Divine Substance and Heavenly Light from the Creator, for it is He who represents the concealed Source behind them that is utterly beyond human comprehension. Still, these radiations constitute a glow reflecting His Divine Essence that is fixed within the limits of man's capacity to partake of and delight in It. To this end it is said in the Talmud: "They rejoice in the Light of the Divine Presence."

This glow itself is an aggregation of all the Lights, which are drawn according to an appropriate course. It is by means of this glow that acts are manifested which in turn give rise to His attributes. In any case, His attributes correspond to the various actions or supervisions wrought by His Lights.

There are ten Lights and it is in the form of a decade that all their functions are arranged. We can discern various types of Lights according to what they effect, as well as from their connections and interrelationships. It is all this that we expound in the wisdom of the *Kabbalah*.

From this collectivity of manifold Lights, together with their branches, there issues an offspring, which is the whole of this known creation together with its laws. Moreover, this manifested creation itself is the completed model of the collectivity of manifold Lights which effected it. Thus, the different parts of creation parallel the various Lights in all their details, and they act as vessels for the various Lights. A relationship exists between Light and vessel in accord with the bestowal of God's bounty and the degree of illumination.

From these Lights, different created beings in nature draw their actual qualities and essences in accordance with their needs, and because of the relationship between Lights and created being, we employ the same terminology for both. Nonetheless, the *Sefirot* are not at all like the created beings, but rather possess certain functions which are germane to their constitution, much like human functions, which are likewise patterned according to human nature.

Thus, for example, we talk of "speech" between one *Sefira* and another, or we say that they "embrace" each other, and so on. But here speech means a certain type of connection which partially binds one *Sefira* with another in that one illumination that has been issued from a fixed boundary may enter the boundary of another illumination.   The offspring of such a link in the *Sefirot* manifests amidst humans as speech, which issues from the speaker to the listener.

All the other functions which take place in the upper Lights may be similarly understood to apply to functions in man, for they are one and the same, each manifesting according to the laws of their own particular nature. Perfection, or emendation, is the offspring, or result of the appropriate ascents upward on the ladder of being.

Chapter Two

Zimzum

Zimzum means that the Creator, blessed be He, has hidden, or contracted His goodness in the act of creating His beings. This was done in order to produce imperfect beings, even so far as the human standard is concerned. How much greater, in relation to His standard, is the imperfection of the human design!

Chapter Three

The Worlds

The worlds that were created in the center of the Infinite, blessed be He, are a collective arrangement comprising everything pertaining to all created being, for the purpose of proving the truth of His unity. There is a continual ascent in all creation until the truth of His unity is inevitably disclosed. For this unity is the central point that proves the infinite virtues of His perfection, and it is around this goal that all creation revolves.

We find then that the orderly sequence of all the worlds is arranged for the single purpose of unveiling the Creator's unity, which at first is concealed, but which will finally be revealed.

Chapter Four

Place

What is meant by place is that the Creator makes room for beings to exist, and that He sustains them. This is manifested by the Creator's own desire, for His pure eternal being left no room for anything outside Himself. Since He decreed existence for created being, He devised a place for it so that at the very moment of the decree, and no sooner, the opportunity for creation to exist was born. And once room was provided for the existence of created beings, it was necessary that they come into being in order to fill the vacated space, for without them, space would remain a vacuum.

This condition was produced by evolving degrees: first the place itself, that is, the vacuum, which sufficed to contain the entire creation, was created. Then beings in whom the order of supervision exists as a source, came into existence.

Chapter Five

The Line of Light and The Impression

The Impression of Light is the power which remained when the Infinite Light was withdrawn as a source for the world and the *Sefirot* from the middle point. When compared to what has been withdrawn, it is but a faint impression of Light. If not for the contraction (*zimzum*) mentioned earlier, the world would have been created in accordance with the undiminished Light. This *Impression* of Light is the source of the lower beings who appear in their incomplete (fallible) state. It is the root of everything pertaining to good and evil, which issue in a state of balanced power, and denote a condition contrary to total perfection.

The Line of Light is the perfection which the Creator, blessed be He, returns to the Impression. It comprises in its supervision the bounty that completes that which is lacking in all existing beings. This completion however only relates to the capacities of created beings, and not to the absolute perfection of the Creator Himself. For He hovers above all as the Infinite Encircling Light.

This perfection of the created being brought by the Line of Light merely fulfills the potential inherent in all that partakes of the nature of the Impression. It was the Creator's desire to fashion two distinct creations: one of deficiency and another of perfection, so that the cycle of deficiency shall have sole away at times. But His final intention is to perfect that which is imperfect. Hence the supervision of good and evil operates openly, while the supervision of perfection operates in a concealed manner: the hidden governing power of completeness underlies those processes which operate secretly towards the goal of perfecting all things, freeing them from evil, and bringing them to a condition of total goodness.

The Impression is designated as "primordial atmosphere" (*awir kadmon*) since it comprises all that pertains to the government of good and evil in a collective form. That is, there is as yet no subdivision into parts and attributes each according to its appointed function. Everything is but in a tenuous root form.

However, when the Line of Light entered the Impression it took charge of everything pertaining to it and arranged that very substance into attributes. It arranged collective attributes and individual ones, each suited to a particular need of the government, and became identified with the collectively, in its extremely tenuous form, of all that pertains to the supervision.

The attributes, or all the *Sefirot* and the vessels, are those very things which were inherent in the Impression. But now (because of the entry of the Line of Light) they subdivide, issue, and assume sway over creation. At this point, each attribute becomes a single vessel. This process was executed by the Line of Light, since all acts

are rooted in and related to it, just as the actions of a
body are related to the soul, which motivates the movements of the body. But the soul only executes those
actions of which the vessels of the body are capable, and
she operates, by means of each member of the body,
according to its inherent capacity.

Similarly, every action that pertains to the Impression
is brought into effect by the power of the Line of Light.
In the human body, the soul has authority to perform
still another function, namely, the purification of the
corporeal matter of the body. This corresponds to a
second function of the Line of Light, which operates in
the Impression to the end that perfection shall triumph
over imperfection and thus bring the whole process of
government to completion.

From the beginning, the substance of the emendations, corresponding to the flaw which they were to
correct, formed a root in the Impression. But the build-
ing of the vessels themselves only effected through the
Line of Light, just as in the case of the body, where all
that pertains to it, including its own functioning, depends on the soul. Therefore the beginning of the emendation concerns the Impression; or the body itself;
and the final stage of the emendation will occur when
the soul will actually encircle it.

The Line of Light which descends from the Infinite
into the vacuum is like a tenuous tube through which the
Light from the Emanator descends to the emanated
being, and it is by means of this Line of Light that Emanator and emanated being are united. All actions
executed by the Creator are in accord with His per-

fection; he decrees th measure by means of which His acts shall affect us, but the procedure remains impercetible to man. His acts reach us through the very boundaries which He appointed for that purpose, and we find that the Creator in His exalted perfection does everything. The "Small Path" in which the Light is modified into a single limited Line of Light, becomes the place where Creator (God) and His created beings can meet.

By assuming this fixed limitation, the Creator converts the act into the governing power that represents unity—referred to above as the rule of good alone. It is this limited act itself that administers the laws pertaining to the Impression. Should the deeds come down to us just as the Creator Himself executes them, everything would be different; of course it is impossible for us even to picture such actions. But since His acts themselves reach us only after having been modified by these limited boundaries which He prepared for us, therefore, nothing is produced by these actions but that is within the bounds of the Impression and the Line of Light.

However the unity between the Emanator and the first emanated being is so great that even *its* emanated *Sefirot* are related to the Infinite, Who acts in them according to His own perfection. When His act comes into the "small path" it infuses the *Sefirot* with enough of His exaltedness to empower them with the supervision of the worlds that leads to the ultimate unity of all.

Chapter Six

The Infinite Light

When the Infinite Light entered the world of Emanation it was divided in two, that is, into the Inner Light and the Encircling Light.

All actions, both good and evil, are rooted in the vessels, the attributes of the reigning government of the world. However, from the standpoint of the governing power of unity (which works secretly in conjunction with the outer government) the hidden intent of every act proceeding from Him is nothing but good. And on that future day when the glory of God will be revealed to all, the prophet's words: "O Lord I will praise Thee though Thou wast angry with me" will have real meaning, for then it will be known that all was for the good.*

However, even when His goodness will be disclosed, the full depth of His workings, will not be revealed. For they will broaden by degrees and increase greatly. Thus, what will be known immediately upon revelation of the truth—which is the very least of what may be known— is rooted in the Inner Light which is confined to the limits of the vessel. But what there is still in store, that is, the greater part of the wisdom, ultimately to be revealed in ever greater measure, like a deed whose effects are of ever widening scope, is rooted in the Encircling Light which expands outside the vessel.

Chapter Seven

Ten Internal and Ten External Sefirot

Out of ten internal and ten external *Sefirot*, Adam Kadmon was fashioned. This creation denotes the existence of two types of supervision: one, the "mode of the Shining Countenance," the other the "mode of the Concealed Countenance", from these two, perfection and imperfection are drawn into the government of the worlds, while in the created being, they affect the soul and the body. When the body dominates, then imperfection has sway, and the government is functioning through the Concealed Countenance—to the extent that man has allowed his body sway. But when the soul dominates, then perfection has sway to the extent that man allows his soul to rule.

There are two distinct modes of supervision in the sequential order, each with its definitely fixed laws. They represent respectively the Line of Light, and the Impression. When they are united and intermingled, the resulting perfection eliminats fallibilities. At this point it is the combination of Light and Impression in unity and completion that governs the worlds. From both of these, as a composite of internal and external, Adam Kadmon is produced.

The principal government of the world is the off-spring which issues from this union of Light and Impression for the government was only established after this union was already consummated. It is in accord with this combination of Line and Impression that the government is established for all time, but it is variable so that at first it will spring from the ruling Line of Light, or the internal Light, then again, when *they* triumph, it will spring from the ruling vessels, or the external Light. Either supervision is nevertheless achieved through the combination of the two governing powers. This offspring (or supervising power) constitutes the branches of Adam Kadmon, which are all issued after the internal and external Lights have already united.

---

* Isaiah XII, 1.

Chapter Eight

The Branches of The Archetypal Man

The branches of Adam Kadmon are the worlds fashioned from the Lights which issued by way of his hair and his sense organs, and represent the super-visions that were fixed following the union of internal and external Lights. Lights containing submerged vessels inhabit these issuing radiations. Because they are submerged, the vessels are rendered inactive and impotent under the immense force of the Light. However since the Lights are issued downward by way of the vessels, they inevitably carry along with them some of the substance of which these vessels themselves consist, until eventually a vessel is fashioned in them.

The presence of characters (letters) points either to the presence of a vessel or to the source of one. Thus, in the Lights which bear the Name of 72, there is no mention of any letter whatsoever, for the type of vessels that belongs there are completely submerged in the Light. This absence of letters precludes any mention of vessels.

In the Lights of the Ear of Adam Kadmon, one *He'* is mentioned which becomes the general source for the vessel to be revealed.

In the Lights of this Nose, six *Alefs* are mentioned. This means that a vessel of a mist tenuous nature is beginning to manifest. But all this is still only preparatory to its actual manifestation.

In the Lights of his mouth, four *Alefs* are mentioned, for then was the coarsest most tangible form of the vessel revealed. Moreover, as a result of the clashing of the Lights outside of the Mouth, all twenty-two letters are revealed; thus manifesting all aspects pertaining to the being of a vessel. The return of these Lights of the Mouth to their source, or their concealment, affects the actual existence of a vessel. Nevertheless, the vessel is only accessory to the Lights, in that it is one to their ten; and they have the power to sustain and greatly illumine the vessel by their strength.

However, in the Lights of the Eyes, there are ten vessels, paralleling the ten Lights. In this case the Lights do not have so much power to shine into the vessel and to emend them, for here each part of the vessel already possesses a strong power of dominion with which to resist the purification imposed upon them by the Lights.

Nevertheless, prior to the shattering of the vessels, the Lights had not as yet abandoned them. But when the shattering occurred, the Lights completely vacated the vessels, causing them to break, and revealing their latent corruption. Even after the vessels were later emended, the original break remained. Until complete emendation takes place, when all will be as it was prior to the shattering of the vessels, (indeed, as though they had never been broken), a literal Pandora's Box full of reptiles will always menace man by hanging constantly behind his back. The Kingdom will only be complete when the perfect emendation is achieved, then a primordial innocence will once again pervade the world.

All these processes constitute the source of the conditions governing man's essential state, for he is composed of two elements body and soul. When the body rules, it counts as a defect for the soul, and the lack of emendation in the soul increases in proportion to the degree of domination on the part of the body. On the other hand, the soul achieves its elevation in the exact measure that the body loses dominion. Under the present supervision in which the body is given dominion the soul remains debased. This condition exists in order that man be subject to the evil *yezer*. But at the end of this era of choice, the soul will be empowered to rise from its low estate to triumph over the body, to purify it in successive stages, until its transformation is so complete that the two may unite as one.*   At this perfect union, all possible bodily defects will vanish. Illumined by the Light of the soul, and utterly bound to it, the corporeal part of man will finally return to unite with its source. This ultimate communion requires a tremendous and awesome effort, for here and now, in our mundane world, the body dominates and is "master of the house" while the soul is in "a strange land." Moreover, man's corporeal nature— which at the very least could have been emended and

---

* TR. N. Although the body has dominion because of its accessibility to the "evil inclination", man still has the free will to choose his path of action.

freed from corruption, is now as corrupt as the beast in the field. This condition has its roots in the state of the worlds following the shattering. The descent, the shattering, and the corruption of the primordial Kings provided the source for the decadence and corruption in man and in his deeds.

In his emended state, however, corporeal man—although his body will still function normally and retain its dominion—will be pure, holy and similar in his functioning to the priests in the Holy Temple when they partook of the sacrifices and fulfilled various divine services. This condition has its source in the world of Points prior to the shattering, and it is this emendation that will prevail at the time of resurrection. The body and this source will then be in the same state, as they were prior to the shattering. This condition implies an enormous purification of the body's corporeality. Yet this is still considered to be corporeal functioning, for the bodies would continue to inhabit the mundane world, as this does not by any means involve the idea of total regeneration of the world. That, says the sages, will only occur at the elapse of the year 7000.

The second degree of perfection occurs when the body begins to relinquish its dominance. That is, though none of its powers will be annulled, it will be elevated by the power of the soul, and the roles will be reversed: Now the soul will be "Lord", and the body "stranger in the land." Similarly when Moses rose up to Heaven he did not lose his human powers, yet his behavior was no different from that of the angels. Further proof of this principle is exemplified by the Angels who came to

Abraham. They certainly did not lose their spiritual estate, but they acted no differently from the inhabitants of the land.

Moses' nature was corporeal, while that of the Angels was spiritual; the partaking of food by the Angels, and the abstaining from food in the part of Moses, are both governed by the same principle—namely, that the individuals were outside of their realm, and that they acted in accordance with the custom of the new one without forfeiting their own nature. So it will be during the era of the years 6000-7000, when the world is still not regenerated. There will be no need for any change in the laws governing the body, but, the Creator, blessed be He, will make wings for the righteous with which they shall soar over the "face of the waters." The sanctity of the soul will sustain the weight of the corporeality, so that the righteous will not be encumbered by material considerations of the yet unregenerated world.

This higher degree of perfection has its source in the Bound World (*Olam Ha-akudim*), where there is actually a vessel and therefore a body. But here the body is carried and sustained by the power of the extended Lights which are "master of the house" wherein the single vessel (containing all the vessels of the Bound World) is the transient guest.

The regeneration of the whole world will follow this cycle. Then the body will lose its nature, and its defects will vanish, leaving the soul itself to rule. First it will be necessary for the body to relinquish its crudest state, to remain within the realm of the world of the Nose. Here where there are only six *Alefs*, it will wait

until it gradually begins to lose even its finer traits.
Only the general source of bodily forces, wherein there
is no subdivision into particular powers, will remain with
it. For it is a prevailing rule that in all things there is
the general (which is the source) and the particular
(the branch). This higher condition in the world of
the Ear, which contains only one letter—*He'*, will prevail
until the body begins to rid itself of even this degree of
corporeality, eliminating any further cause of darkness
to the soul. At this phase the body will be totally sub-
jugated, no more than an accessory to the soul, which
will then shine perfectly in all its aspects. This condition is
apparently derived from the source corresponding to the
Light of the Hair which, to us, is entirely imperceptible;
for we can have no conception whatsoever of that place
wherein there is no origin of body.

Chapter Nine

The World of Points

The World of Points is the source for the truth of the Creator's unity, which can only be disclosed through Light contrasting with darkness. In this particular world, therefore; the source of evil can be found in both its aspects: first as actual evil, and second in its potential inversion to good.

Like this one, all the worlds which are divided into two categories, exist in order to reveal the unity of the Creator which inhabits their center. At the start it is necessary to verify the truth of His unity, by means of a gradual process of unfoldment which ranges from its total concealment in darkness to its final revelation in Light. Once the truth itself is clearly established, a progression of elevation is rendered to the souls, enabling them to understand the profound matters and mighty perceptions pertaining to this truth.

These events take place during two periods that cover first the concealment and then the revelation. The four worlds known as A'B'Y'A (Emanation, Creation, Formation and Action) provide the setting, which operates during the period when the truth is still concealed, and the process of clarification is in progress. In

Adam Kadmon, the worlds from the Mouth up are those in which the period of revelations takes place. Here, once the truth is established, the Creator, blessed be He, renders exalted perceptions to the rejoicing souls of His righteous ones.

Chapter Ten

The Primordial Kings: Their Shattering

The general source of nature as we know it, including all of its destructive forces lies in the world and in the shattering of the Primordial Kings. When we refer here to nature, we do not mean the species, but rather the abstract qualities of Nature herself.

After the shattering of the vessels came the emendation. And then the attributes (*Sefirot*) of good, from which all evil was expelled, were fashioned on the one hand, while the evil which was expelled from them made up the *Sefirot* of the "other side", also known the husks. Then, according to its latent predisposition, nature implanted its species admixture of good and evil, as befitted them.

The Primordial Kings represent the origins of existing nature in its imperfect state and not as it will be in the time to come, when there will be a "new heaven and a new earth." In keeping with this imperfect existence, the Creator decreed the annulment which brought about the shattering that became the source of all destructive force.

For the perfect existence, the Creator decreed no annulment. Everything pertaining to the perfect emendation of the future has its roots above. Then all defects caused by the shattering will be thoroughly emended, and nothing in nature will ever suffer any annulment. Thus it is written: "For as the new Heavens and the new earth, which I will make shall remain before me, said the Lord . . ." (Isaiah LXVI, 22).

The Creator only fashioned an incomplete source so that evil might come into existence in order to test man. He therefore fashioned the Kings incompletely according to the incompleteness of evil.

Because the source of the evil spirit or husk sprung from the Primordial Kings, they were neither arranged in parallel pillars, nor united with the feminine polarity. In addition they lacked all the other emendations which are now in effect in the world of Emanation.

As long as the Creator holds united in His grasp the two modes of supervision, that is, the "mode of the shining Countenance" and the "mode of the Concealed Countenance", there is no corruption, and no destruction, in existence; for corruption and darkness only come into existence when He completely conceals His Face from the world. At that point all the demons and degrees of defilement come into being. This is conveyed in the phrase "death of the Kings", meaning that the Lights departed, leaving only vessels which serve as the roots of the defects, that deprive the world of perfection. From the supervision of the "Concealed Face" issued the husk (or *Sitra ahara*) and all that springs from it.

There is an expression in the *Zohar* to the effect that "the Master struck the iron with a hammer and brought out sparks." This refers to the Creator, Who issued degrees and numerous large worlds, all of which he bound into man by means of deep ties and big chambers or cells, like the complicated mechanism of a watch. His primary purpose in all this was to effect complete goodness and perfect emendation in His creatures.

However in these chambers there is also evil, which also exists for the ultimate promulgation of the good. Those constituents that are intrinsically good are designed for eternal dominion, whereas the evil is made to be subdued and overcome. Thus, though we find that evil in itself is nothing more than monstrous corruption and absolute loss, when it is introduced into the sum total of the chambers, it too becomes converted to good. It therefore serves no purpose other than that of being overcome and bearing witness to the unity of God. However, since all is newly created from Him, and there is nothing holy that is not the Creator Himself to begin with, this evil, of necessity, had to be devised just as it was in its first stage. When it is connected with the other contents in the chambers, it can be converted. So that when the Supreme Thought proceeds to emend the image of man (the sum total of all the chambers) He first brings forth the whole of evil itself and the entire scope thereof, including all the damaging agents comprised in the Primordial Kings. The Creator's intention for them was only that they incur annulment in existing being.

Thereafter the Supreme Thought brings forth the remaining chambers and joins evil with them so that evil might be subdued and not, itself, subdue. In this way evil too enters in as one of those causes that effect complete good in man, by reason of having been vanquished by it, and thereby bearing witness to the unity of God

Note that everything pertaining to evil is comprised in the *Sefirot* of the Name 52, the world of Points. The origin of the existence of imperfect beings is in the reign of the Primordial Kings. The origin of the annulment of existent being is in the annulment of the Kings. Everything that came into existence anew through their annulment constitutes the source of all destruction and loss that is found in nature. The sum total of all the good chambers are comprised in the image of man.* When the essence of evil is connected with these chambers for the sole purpose of being vanquished, it too will convert into goodness for all time. This connotes the emendation of the Name 52 through the Name 45, and means also that the origin of darkness and evil will revert to good, since it stands ready to receive the emendation of the Name 45, and to reject the dominion of evil.

Remember that the Thought of the Creator from the start was aimed at making room for the existence of evil, and for that reason He issued imperfect origins for existent being. But now (at the time of emendation) He intends that darkness and evil revert to good. Then He will regenerate all these imperfect beings, bringing them to greater perfection than ever. The origins for both imperfect and perfect beings were devised in the *Sefirot* that were fashioned following the emendation.

---

* TR. N. By "man" the author refers to the Name 45 which has the numerical value of Adam (man), and which was issued for the purpose of emending the Name 52 by uniting with it.

Chapter Eleven

The Shattering And Fall of The Primordial Kings

The shattering and fall of the Primordial Kings constitute two evils: one is corruption and loss, and the other is debasement. You may see an intimation of the break-up of the seven Primordial Kings (or vessels) in the last two acrostics of the Hebrew verse of the opening section of the daily morning prayers (*tof zadi*) which reads *taz*. The acrostic of the entire Hebrew verse reads *abgitaz.**

The descent of the hind part of Father and Mother was different and this is indicated in the acrostic of the verse following the one previously quoted: *Kuf, Resh, 'Ayin, Sin, Tet, Nun,* which reads *kra' Satan.*** The esoteric significance of this prayer is supplied in other Kabbalistic writings.

The difference between the damage done to the Primordial Kings and that of the hind parts of Father and Mother is that the breaking of the seven lower

---

* TR. N. The word *taz* itself means "breaking". In English, this verse reads as follows: "O Lord we beseech thee to loosen with the greatness of Thy powerful right hand those that are bound in captivity."

** " Accept the cry of thy people. Exault and purify us O thou Who are tremendous."

Sefirot (the Primordial Kings)—because of their descent, to the world of Creation—was most complete, for it entailed absolute shattering. Their descent is called "complete death", while the descent of the hind part of Father and Mother is merely an annulment.

The Primordial Kings were the sources of that exalted stage to which the worlds, together with all that existed in them could have attained, namely that stage to which man and the world could have risen if not for the fall of the first Adam. When the shattering occurred it meant that whatever was drawn from the vessels was annulled, and that the vessels could no longer serve as sources to existent being. Thus, in the absence of the source, the offspring which derives therefrom is inevitably eliminated. This fact itself caused debasement of these sources. Had they not been shattered, their glory would have been increased by their having been the sources for good things. But their glory is decreased along with the cessation of their dominion and the annulment of their efficient functioning as sustainers of offspring. This is the meaning of the verse in the Torah: "Of the Rock that begat thee thou art mindful." (Deut. XXXII, 18). According to the sages: "The Rock which gave you birth is weakened . . ."

Debasement results from lack of dominion and signifies nothing but annulment. This means that the fallen one remains in the world which he had previously inhabitd—only in a lower degree. He does not depart from that world. The "hind parts" mentioned earlier exemplify this condition in that they did not leave the world of Emanation, and therefore cannot be connected with death, but rather with inaction, or annulment.

However in the case of the seven lower ones (the Primordial Kings), there is additional debasement. The Creator desired to lower them from one world to the next so that they descended into the worlds of Creation, Formation, and Action. This conveys how completely they have changed their places and their original loftiness. The change entailed a different law and a different mode of action; this is what is actually meant by "debasement of the worlds."

This primordial debasement is comparable to the principle at work in the creation of Adam, the first to be created in a non-exalted stage of perfection, but only with the potentiality of attaining that loftiness in the fuure that is, if he were not to sin.

With the descent of these Sefirot into Creation, Formation, and Action, the effects of the break increased in that the immense and powerful sources of corruption took root in them. They then acquired the full might of evil to such an extent that death became related to them, the Kings. However this matter of shattering was no accident, no incidental occurence, for it was the intention of the Supreme Thought to effect what actually took place at the time of the shattering. The shattering was not extensive in the hind parts of Father and Mother, for they descended only within the world of Emanation itself, and corruption was not much increased in them. They are related to annulment, but not to death. In his inferior status, man is subject to great corruption; for had Adam been created in his perfect state, that evil which attempted to dominate him would not have triumphed.

Prior to the shattering the place of the Sefirotic worlds was within the degree of Emanation, ranging downward from the navel of its feminine polarity. But when those *Sefirot* lost their superior status and continued to remain merely at the levels of Creation, Formation and Action, the worlds also descended to the soles of the feminine polarity, the location for the three lower worlds of *Beria, Yetzira, Assiah* (B'Y'A). Although later they returned and rose so that the entire worlds of *Atziluth, Beriah, Yetzira,* and *Assiah* (A'B'Y'A) were formed out of them, they never really rose to assume their original degree in the first world of Emanation.

It is evident then that the worlds of B'Y'A are no more than what is drawn from the Emanation that was formed after the advent of the shattering, and not from the original Emanation. Moreover, they did not return to their original place, for they only gained *some* elevation, and not a complete one at that. This is why the Name 63 was converted into the Name 52 and is no longer called 63. In the future, when all the worlds will actually return to their original exalted degrees, the Name 52 will once more be 63.

The first and second falls of the vessels may be explained as follows: The whole of *B'Y'A* were made only from the seven lower *Sefirot* of the world of Points, since the first three, did not leave the world of Emendation. However, the truth is that, following the Emendation, all *Parezufim* of the world of Emanation, are also formed out of the selections of the seven broken lower Sefirot. This was possible bcause the worlds had not returned to their original degrees. These seven *Sefirot* must therefore be subdivided into ten in order to establish all the *Sefirot* for *B'Y'A,* including in them the necessary

states of density and obscurity required for the purposes
of good and evil.   The ten *Sefirot* of the world of Emanation itself were completed from these seven.   And so,
developing ten *Sefirot* out of seven required two falls.

With the first fall, only the head of the world of
Creation was established.   Of everthing residing within
the worlds it is the most complete, for there the Light
still precedes the vessels.   But through the second fall,
the rest of the world was established, and this was more
obscure because the Light is already at a considerable
distance from the vessels.   A basic requirement for all the
worlds is that the head be at a distance from the body.
That is, in all places the head must be exalted and more
elevated than the rest of the body, no matter which
degree it occupys—the world of Emanation or the worlds
of B'Y'A, the *Sefirot* or the created being.

In view of the place to which the vessels descended,
it was possible to establish ten Sefirot of *Beria, Yetzira,
Assiah* (*B'Y'A*), and because they themselves were
divided into ten places, it was even possible for that world
of Emanation which followed the emendation to be established.   There the seven *Sefirot* themselves were divided into all ten *Sefirot*.   We find then that the world
of Emanation and those of B'Y'A (which appared after
the emendation), are properly interrelated in their substance.

Chapter Twelve

The Position of The Sefirot

When we speak of one *Sefira* as being located below another, or parallel to another, we are referring respectively to the progression which exists in the created beings (they are arranged in an order where one is higher than the other and where there are still higher ones above them); and to the bonds and relationships between them. In the latter case the *Sefirot* draw together in an attempt to complete an incomplete form, incomplete because it lacks the requisite union of all parts.

The completion of creation calls for a synthesis of all its parts to be the point where individual units are all transformed into a single assemblage of complementary forces. (A complete vessel is similarly made from the gathering of all the Sefirotic parts). For as long as they remain separate entities, created beings will remain subject to corruption and destruction. Emndation will result only when they are gathered together by the Whole, their Creator.

At the outset the Creator issued the *Sefirot* only as a series of successive stages, and not as a co-extensive assemblage of complementary factors. This form automatically decreed for this graded series; consequently, He

arranged the Sefirot in the form of a co-existensive as-
sembly. The whole of the emendation is dependent on
this latter arrangement, in equipoise. Here the *Sefirot*
are like scale, united because they parallel each other, with
the right pillar opposite the left and the center pillar
balancing the two.

As long as this arrangement of pillars continues they
are considered to be inextricably united by virtue of
their parallelism and by the Line of Light radiating
through them.

Chapter Thirteen

Kingdom-The Seventh Sefira

The six *Sefirot* of the Points were not united with "Kingdom", so that no mention is made of a "wife" except in the case of the King called Hadar. That is because all the emendations of bestowal are in effect only when the Bestower turns with love to the recipients. Chief of these are the Divine Presence (the *Shekinah*) or the congregation of Israel as it is conveyed in the Song of Solomon: "I am my beloved's and his desire is toward me." (Song of Solomon, VII, 11). It is Israel who says "I am my beloved's", signifying that she is wholy devoted to the Creator. Only so can she expect that "His desire"—that is, His will to extend bounty—shall extend toward her. For then love increases and dominates to such a degree that all the gates of compassion are opened and all goodness flows forth.

Absence of bestowal is due to the absence of love; that signifies the turning away of the Creator, God forbid, from His recipients, a condition which implies that all the gates of goodness are locked. The Primordial Kings existed in such a state, since the Creator had already foreseen the deeds of the wicked and had decreed fitting punishment for them. But the emendation signifies that the Creator has removed the deeds of the wicked, and, foreseeing the deeds of the righteous, has turned with love to the created ones. He has therefore the highest good for them, according to their merit.

From this act of "turning with love" is drawn the sum total of all the emendations.

Chapter Fourteen

The Two Hundred and Eighty-Eight Sparks

The 288 Sparks signify that the Creator does not permit absolute annulment of existing beings. Thus He sustains them in that very condition of annulment until they receive the full emendation. This is related to the resurrection of man, in whose case an iota of energy remains in the bones of the body for the purpose of maintaining it against total disintegration. This continues up to the time when the Creator returns and builds a new construction.

Note that despite His concealment of His Countenance and the ensuing annulment, the Creator does not slumber, He radiates a minute measure of Light even when His Countenance is concealed so as to preserve the existence of the Created Beings.

Chapter Fifteen

Selection of Sparks Made for The Purpose of The Emendation

We have stated previously that the Upper Powers (i.e. the roots of the world of Points) were annulled. This corresponded to the Creator's intention to manifest evil through them. (Recall that it is the corruption of the roots that produces all the evils in the creation.) But at the time of the emendation it was necessary to regenerate those very powers so that they might again serve as roots through which beings would issue. This could be performed simply by emending the original powers in which annulment had occurred. This is done to permit evil to enter the forces of emendation so that evil may at some point be subdued itself. Hence, the powers of the world of Points serve on the one hand to produce evil, and on the other, to vanquish it.

From this point on it is necessary to separate each power from its manifest destructive force. To begin with, this separation provides each power with the renewed function from which it was originally deprived as a result of the annulment is its actual functioning, which develops in such a way that evil is no longer drawn from it, and is instead distantly removed from its nature. Indeed, if the intention had been to eliminate the evil from the world, the Creator would have cancelled evil entirely, but since He desired that it remain in existence, it was necessary for Him to separate it from the powers and their functions, but not to cancel it. He also left a source or root which sustains it and is destined to last until evil is entirely annulled and the words of the prophet are fulfilled: "Death will be annihilated for all eternity."

From the very beginning then, all the *Sefirot* in the world of the Points possessed the capacity to issue evil, so that the source of evil is high indeed, issuing as it does from these exalted degrees. When these roots of evil are emended, however, they lose their capacity to issue for the corruption and become instead the roots of a darkness which is capable of being emended through Light, thereby transforming evil into good. At the completion of this process no room is left for the evil which leads to corruption and which constitutes the actual collectivity of shells themselves. The means of inverting evil to good are all that is left, for evil must be exorcised. The world of Points is the last degree of "Kingdom" in the world of Action. It is no longer included with the other emended degrees, but is instead lowered from one degree to the next until it lands at the lowest of all levels, the collective hind part of the Divine Spirit, and root of the husk. The chief part in this procedure belongs to the last degree of the *Sefira* "Kingdom" in the world of Action. It is that entity which receives absolutely no illumination whatsoever from the upper Line of Light. Of her it is said: "It is necessary to rescue the robbbed from him who robs," for at present she sustains all the evils that parallel the aspects of Divinity.

This operation pleases the Maker because the shell is being expelled from the upper sources, even though it necessitates the expulsion of "Kingdom" from the exalted degrees. Simultaneous with the process of selection and emendation of the degrees of Divine Spirit is the process of forcing down evil and eliminating its hold on the exalted roots. Thus the dross remains finally with the nether beings alone; it descends cumulatively from one *Sefira* to the next, all the way down to the end of the world of Action. Only when the emendation of the divine degrees is completed, will the debasement of evil be accomplished.

Chapter Sixteen

Fashioning of The Vessel

The vessel is fashioned from the selections of the Primordial Kings both in the upper and the lower worlds. The Creator, devised a type of Light encompassing all the *Sefirot* that would answer the needs of the nether beings. In this Light he produced paths and new laws which provide roots for the new beings in nature that are mentioned from the event of the contraction on.

The Primordial Kings contained in themselves all the Lights which were to be revealed in the future worlds of A'B'Y'A.* These Lights were to answer the requirements of the 6000-year cycle. The Primordial Kings represent a source for all those severed beings that will ultimately issue from them. But the Lights themselves comprise the actuality of all these beings; for both alike are Lights too, but in the source the severed beings are comprised only potentially, until later when both Lights and severed beings manifest from them. Still, the newly-devised Lights of the *Sefirot* are nothing but the roots or sources of whatever is found in the severed beings.

---

* TR. N. *Azilut* (Emanation), *Beriah* (Creation), *Yezirah* (Formation) and *Asiah* (Action).

Thus the Creator, blessed be He, devised but one substance responsible for producing the rays in *Sefirot* as well as fashioning the created beings that occupy the severed worlds. Hence it follows that this substance, in all its divisions, is comprised in the Primordial Kings. It is this substance that issues along with the evolving *Sefirot* and fashions the Lights. It is this substance which is later issued in the severed ones and which fashions the created beings.

This is analogous to a situation in which one who conceives the idea of drawing a certain picture, does so in thought alone. Finally the picture itself actually issues from his thought on to paper. It is all one matter, but the difference is that in his thought he makes a mental picture, while on the paper it is an actual drawing.

The Masculine Feminine World

Z'O and upwards represents the masculine domain, while "Kingdom" and below constitute the feminine domain. The former comprises the general laws governing bestowal, the latter the laws governing the recipients.

Macroprosopus and Macroprosopus

These two *Parezufim* in general are the chief factors in the administration governing the world of Emanation. These supervisions correspond respectively to the measure of the Creator's love and to His dispensation of judgment. All the supervisory functions in Z'O are to be understood as the Creator's measure of judgment and all that may be discerned in supervision of *Arik* is to be understood as the Creator's love. The mitigations that *Arik* works on Z'O mean that the Creator's love is tempering His judgments. It is like the father who punishes his son but with the love which is hidden in his heart.* There are mitigations which utterly eliminate

---

* TR. N. Z'O receives bounty from the Source for the purpose of governing and maintaining all the lower worlds and man. This bounty is a composite of Mercy and Judgment. The nature of the divine *Parezufim* is ever to bestow and govern the world and man by Mercy. However, the government and bestowal of Z'O to man is conditioned by the deeds of man himself. When man's actions are in accord with the law and order of the Law (Torah) then Mercy and goodness issue from Z'O and then power and joy reign in the world. But if man is corrupt in his behaviour, then Z'O is compelled to exercise wrath and Judgment to all.

Judgment, as for example in the event of the manifestation of the *Mezah Ha-rozon* (the will to good or Mercy, which emanates from the Forehead.)   At other times Judgment remains, but it is tempered. This happens when together with the remaining emendations the Countenance, of *Arik* (Macroprosopus) is manifest.

These mitigations take place because of the love which is natural in a father and which causes him to deal gently with his son, so that even when he punishes him, his blows are not those of an enemy. And again, when the occasion demands it is his love which causes him to suspend judgment entirely.

Chapter Nineteen

Union, Gestation, Birth

These three conditions, mentioned in connection with the *Sefirot*, denote varying aspects of the Lights which the Creator caused to radiate within the created beings. These Lights, governed by law and order, are arranged as interdependent powers all combined, variously interrelated, and forming different aspects of the Lights which are required for the tree of the *Parezufim*.

"Enfoldment" means that the upper *Parezufim* are encompassed by the lower ones, or that the substance of the upper ones is hidden in the interior of the lower ones. At this point we may see that the advantage lies with the enfolded ones, which are concealed, and that the lower *Parezufim*, or those responsible for the enfoldment, react to this process.

The idea of "brain", namely, the last three *Sefirot*— "Triumph", "Glory" and "Foundation"—of an "upper" *Parezuf* which become the brain of the succeeding *Parezuf*, is that in order to complete the lower one it is necessary for a portion of the upper one to enter it. The "inner" brain is the more direct source of a *Parezuf*, while the "encircling" Lights (*the zelem*) are the remoter source.

Our use of the terms "union, gestation and birth" in these discussions of the Light processes is appropriate since all of these stages ramify from each other as cause and effect. So that when one Light, which is a single attribute, issues by the power of two antecedent Lights, it is considered to be caused by them. Thus the initial stage is inevitably an action which results from the meeting of these two Lights. In other words, the two together act to issue their offspring.

When we examine the details of this matter, we see that the subjects and Lights mentioned earlier issue gradually as cause and effect. In them we discern the origin for substance and the origin for form: or in other words, an origin for the general substance and an origin for the specific being. Hence, each attribute or Light is preceded by the two Lights that give it birth. One Light provides its general makeup and substance, the other provides the details in its form.

By these means it is transmitted from the general to the particular cause. Following the union of the two Lights, which is involved in the act of transmission, the offspring issues. This is known as the *union*, that is, when the two Lights connect with each other.

The transmission of the entity from the general cause to the particular one, and the period preceding its actual issuance, that is, while it is still in the particular origin (where it takes on individual identity) is designated gestation or pregnancy. Its actual issuance is designated *birth*.

A closer analysis of the actions of these causes themselves reveals function involving all the *Sifirot* known as "Foundation" and which we call "kissing". Different types of unions must take place between the two causes. They are the functions which are instituted in them in order to produce offspring; for example, there are unions which pertain to the inner Lights—such as kissing, which serves to unite the inner Lights, and there are also unions of the vessels which denote the embrace and the uniting of the "Foundations". These serve to set the vessels parallel to each other, and to combine them in accordance with what is decreed in them.

Finally, when we examine all the parts that are necessary to make up a *Parezuf*—these being the conditions discerned in one of the attributes in its completed stage—we will also understand the unions and combinations which occur in all the parts, and in the parts of those parts. Indeed, according to the particular progression, we will discern still further that even when one of the entities is actually issued, its being is as yet incomplete. Only later does it become complete. This course of development involves the idea of two periods; one immaturity, when an entity must be nourished—for the child needs his mother to nourish him; the other, when it reaches maturity.

That is, the offspring must still attain completion. But its completion comes to it from none other than the very origin which gave it birth.

Chapter Twenty

The Infancy and Maturity of Z'O Father and Mother, Israel The Ancient and Understanding

We have already explained that the *Sefirot* are none other than attributes of the Creator, and that as such they provide channels through which he administers, and paths of Light through which He radiates into His created beings. However He bound these Lights and these supervisions one with the other so that there relationship exists between them.

In addition to what may be known of the content of each one of them according to its function, it is also necessary to know of its relationship to the attributes which either precede or follow it.

Z'O is the aggregate of all the upper Lights, which are the source and cause of all things in this mundane world, in all their details: the qualities of the created beings, as well as the very substance of the different species, their diversified natures, all their laws and their conditions.

The fact is that this mundane world is established on the principle of the Creator's Judgment (the supervision of Z'O). Since He governs the world through the attributes of His Judgment, the offspring partake of the very nature of the *Sefirot*. In other words, His desire is to create a world according to these diverse Lights which represent the sum of His judgmental attributes. For these Lights are drawn in such a manner as to conceal His Goodness, and to reveal instead the rule of Judgment. They are the sum total of all the *Sefirot* of Z'O and from them resulted the creation of this mundane world, in all its subdivisions, and in its present aspect. And since His desire is to govern this creation according to these measures, the existing government of the world appears in all its subdivisions.

Recall that the *Sefirot* are attributes, that they are Lights, and that they constitute sources. They are attributes by reason of their very first function—namely that they serve in God's supervision of His creatures. They exemplify to a certain extent the attributes of the *nefesh* (soul) of man. But the attributes of the Creator are not inherent characteristics in Him, so we only label them modes of action. They are Lights, being none other than the diverse bestowals and various supervisions which are all one and the same thing, emanating from Him: His compassion, His wrath, His righteousness, His meekness, His exaltedness, and so on. And they are indeed sources, since all the different qualities of created being are nothing but offspring from the aggregation of these various supervisions. This may be explained in two ways. First, the quality of the bestowal to the created being matches the nature of the attribute. For the attributes do not administer absolute gain or absolute loss, rather their bestowal is modified according to the different degrees of meritoriousness. Therefore, they discriminate between that which is precious and that which is inferior, between the greater quantity and the lesser quantity, as well as all the other opposing categories discernible in the qualities that are found in the world.

The attribute corresponding to "Compassion" and "Mercy" brings to birth (in the wake of its bestowal) worthiness, Light and abundance; and, conversely, the attribute of wrath and "concealment of Countenane" brings forth, by its bestowal, darkness, degradation and lack. This too is the manner in which the many other paths function.

The second way of explaining this connection of the offspring with its source is as follows: We have already explained that the created beings themselves are exemplifications of the supervision which controls them; similarly, these Lights produce offspring like themselves; or in other words, that resemble the supervision. And so the *Sefirot* are the source.

To pursue the point further, the *Sefirot* of Z'O are the attributes of the Creator's Judgments. They are the sources of the qualities of nature and its denizens. They are the sources for the created beings of this world, which are constructed only according to the prototypes that these *Sefirot* represent. However, we have already explained that what must first be discerned in the *Sefirot* is their function of supervision, namely, attributes (which limit)—after which a larger number of Lights and a larger number of sources are drawn into manifestation. Therefore, we will first discern the content of Z'O, according to its attributes of supervision which represent the measure of Judgment. Thereafter we will examine all that pertains to Z'O as *Sefirot*, Lights and sources.

As we have learned, Z'O is the measure of the Creator's Judgment. It represents the root of the measure of Judgment. Judgment is the result of the concealment of the Creator's goodness. But in the measure of Judgment itself we may discern two types: first severe Judgment, which is wrath, contempt and abandonment; second, emended Judgment, which is tempered Judgment. Hence, Z'O embraces all the varied aspects of Judgment. When we analyze the progression of this Judgment we shall recognize it to be first of all utter, severe Judgment. Following that, we distinguish modification and a trace of emendation in it. Thereafter more modification and more emendation is presented, until it becomes completely perfect.

Note that the first degree of Judgment, wrath and fury, is the condition that brought about the shattering of the vessels in the Primordial Kings. This event is the offspring of absolute Judgment. Soon we note that Z'O is undergoing something of an emendation and a modification. Nevertheless it is still but a slight degree of mitigation. Its offspring is a defective order, namely one in which complete destruction does not take place, as it does in the case of the shattering of the vessels, the offspring of absolute, severe Judgment. Nevertheless in this second defective offspring every good order is corrupted.

This is the time when the Creator's scale of Judgment is unknown in the world. (That is, to the world it will seem as though the Creator's supervision is missing.) On the contrary, of this time the Scriptures say: "And I will surely hide my face in that day . . . and they shall be devoured and many evils and troubles shall befall them. . . ."

(Deut. XXXI, 18, 17). The wicked will be successful and arrogence will increase. The righteous will walk with bowed heads.

Following this we see Z'O receiving still further modification and emendation; at this stage the world will no longer be forsaken. The righteous will enjoy some success, although it will not as yet be complete.

Thereafter we distinguish Z'O as corrected and emended Judgment: here the world contains good judgments for the meritorious and evil judgments for the wicked. Everything is emended in the best possible order.

These three periods distinguished between the immaturity and maturity of Z'O. The immature stage of Z'O is Judgment, but its pre-natal state is unmitigatedly severe Judgment—actual obscurity. In the "nursing" period Judgment is modified. These two stages both represent the Name *Elohim*. Maturity, the stage which denotes more compassion, represents the Name *Havaya*. But even in maturity, Z'O is never other than the measure of Judgment, albeit emended Judgment.

Note that this entire progression of the existing measure of Judgment traces it from its initial stage down to the level where it reaches completion. However, since these Lights issue one from the other in the manner of cause and effect, we must examine this

structure of the measure of Judgment (Z'O) as it issues
from its cause.

The first emendation which is rendered this
attribute (Z'O) from its cause (Mother) supplies
it with a slight degree of modification so that at least
no chaos and destruction (such as occurred in the earlier
case of the Primordial Kings) should result from it. This
first construction containing the design for Z'O was
fashioned in Mother at the time of gestation. As the
cause of Judgment, she herself is obliged to effect this
improvement; she must include in herself everything
that relates to Judgment so that she may impart to it
the necessary modification that will free it from its
destructive state (which is the offspring of untempered
Judgment) and permit it to enter into the emended
condition of the measure of Judgment.

What is required of her at this particular juncture
in the process of emendation is the establishment of
Judgment mingled with a specific measure of Justice, so
that it will no longer be untempered Judgment. When
the cause effected this, she accomplished the first stage
of what she was supposed to do by herself, namely to
temper the untempered Z'O. But her work was still
to be completed.

The first step in tempering Judgment is considered
to take place in the period of gestation. At this stage
Z'O was being built within the Mother, that is, his
Sefirot were selected from out of the chaos of the Primordial Kings and put together inside her. The advantage of this first emendation is only that Z'O emerges

from chaos to the emendation of balance (miskelech.*
However, Judgment still remains severe Judgment, which
implies that all the orders are defective. But at least
in its new condition it is not tantamount to destruction.
Nevertheless, when the period of gestation prevailed in
the general supervision (the first step in Z'O's emendation) then the world was in complete darkness. Even
the Law (Torah) did not appear in the world. In other
words, it is represented in particular by the entire period
of the exile in Egypt, and, in general, by the remaining
2000 years of "chaos".

However, from birth onward, the continual emendations of Z'O begin to accrue to Judgment. These are
the ones that are enacted in him during both the
nursing and the mature periods, that is, all during the
time when Z'O is in the process of being constructed.
Thus the existence of an emended order for ruling
the world is in the process of preparation. But as long
as the process consists only of continual unions of Lights
and the emended order is not fully complete, the supervision (by the emended Z'O) is concealed within the
King's domain and remains entirely unrevealed. This
signifies that Z'O is concealed in Mother and is non-
manifest. For all the preparations of goodness which the
Creator is making for the world during the period of
Z'O growth are, being formed in secret. When the

---

* TR. N. In the Primordial Kings the *Sefirot* of Z'O were
arranged in a single pillar—ranging one below the other, but the
first emendation of balance means that they were arranged in three
parallel pillars.

preparations are complete, the final act occurs—Z'O is born. During the secret preparatory period, however, the first corruption still prevails. Yet, as bad as this order of corruption may be it is still a step away from complete destruction. At this point, although the Creator proceeds to correct the matter, the corruption of order still remains, for during the entire period of preparation in the upper realms, nothing is revealed to the nether beings.

Another point to recall here is that the Creator, blessed be He, is only capable of doing good and that even the period of the concealed Countenance is not due to His having scorned the world. On the contrary, He is secretly preparing emendation for its defects; in the meantime the world suffers many evils and troubles.

To reiterate, we find, on analyzing the government in all its aspects during the period of gestation, that there are three distinct phases: 1) what pertains to Mother; 2) what pertains to the condition of Z'O; 3) what pertains to the immature stage of Z'O.

Thus the period of gestation signifies that the construction of Z'O is going on secretly and that it is achieved through Mother, inside of her. And, simultaneously, with the final emendation of the world as its goal, the state of an emended order is in the process of being prepared. This preparation is not, however, the work of the Mother. She is the cause of righteous Judgment (Z'O) which remains concealed in the upper realms, and, because of her, is not revealed below. What is manifested during that period is the corruption of the good orders. Yet this is not total destruction, whereas

in the state of the first corruption (when the *Sefirot*
of Z'O were all issued in one pillar) final destruction
was wrought in the shattering of the vessels. Here at
least, the Creator assumes the task of emendation so
as to avoid any repetition of shattering. Nonetheless,
the world remains unredeemed, yoked still to the corrupt orders, since its emendation can only come through
the revelation of righteous Judgment (Z'O). But Z'O
itself is concealed, and this condition exists because
the *Sefirot* of Z'O are in the process of being selected;
and, because they are not yet manifest outside of the
feminine polarity (Mother), they cannot assume their
places in the administration. The immaturity (*katnut*)
which precedes each elevation to a higher degree is
considered to be concealed preparation for a new stage
of emendation; here there is no corruption and no darkness.

Up to this point we have been discussing the attributes from the standpoint of their governing order.
But when we analyze them as far as their modes of
bestowals are concerned we shall understand that the
Sefirot of Z'O constitute the sum total of the bestowals
which bring to birth the material things of the mundane
plane.

The Creator's bounty, a bestowal which is drawn
from the divine source, is fit to produce only that which
is of a Godly, spiritual or divine nature. But the Creator,
blessed be He, desired that the quality of His bestowal
should be debased in order to produce the material offspring which He desired. Thus we find that even in
this procedure of bestowal there is the appropriate
gradation.

That is, the bestowal begins from that point which —in accordance with the upper decree—enables it to descend gradually to the level which caters to the requirements of a mundane world. The first radiation emitted by the Creator is of a spiritual and tenuous nature, entirely free from matter;* it produces only offspring of tenuous, Godly and spiritual nature. This is the first type of Light.

Next in the scale of gradually evolving Lights comes a type of Light whose offspring is also Godly and spiritual, yet not entirely free of matter, for it is already combined with matter itself in that it allows its existence. Nevertheless, it is combined in such a way that the Light may shine into its obscurity in the required proportion.

Following this second type of Light comes a third type, wherefrom actual matter is drawn.

The three descending types of Light are:

1) "Crown"
2) "Wisdom" and "Intelligence"
3) The seven lower *Sefirot*

"Crown", the collective *Parezuf* of *Arik,* is free from matter. "Wisdom" and "Intelligence" are drawn successively; they constitute the *Parzuf* of Father and Mother.

---

* TR. N. This is not actually physical matter, but only a spiritual Light, which, in relation to the more tenuous Lights preceding it, is opaque.

Lastly, the seven lower *Sefirot* are the Lights from which matter issues. They constitute the collective *Parezuf* of Z'O and *Nukbah* ("Kingdom"), the former constituting the major part, while the latter is merely the termination of Z'O. This *Parezuf* is the collective Light from which the mundane world issues.

This mundane world is composed both of matter and of Light,—that is, knowledge, intelligence, and other factors pertaining to the soul. Through this power of knowledge and intelligence we can discern the six dimensions in Z'O which are the sources of matter, as well as its first three *Sefirot*, which constitute the brain that reaches Z'O from Father and Mother. Father and Mother represent the second type of Light that combines with matter and has the capacity to impart something of itself—in this case, the varying capacities of "Brain" to Z'O. What is designated as mature or immature, or in states of elevation, refers to the differing quantities of Light which are combined with matter. Here in man they represent the different degrees of worth or merit: the six dimensions are the sources of man's material substance, but the treasure of intelligence which resides within him is rooted in the first three *Sefirot*. Thus, according to the system of evolvement, wherein the Lights issue one from the other as cause and effect, Father and Mother gave birth to Z'O, that is, to his six dimensions and, although his content is different from theirs (for he is the source of matter) they nevertheless produce him just as he is. Still, they impart to him something of their own essence, and it is this that constitutes the first three *Sefirot*.

Such transference is possible only by virtue of the fact that Lights emanate one from the other. If not for this, the world would be wholly corporeal and completely devoid of Spirit or Light.

The brain joins with the attributes (the six dimensions). Note that in the measure of Judgment itself (in Z'O) the Light is of an obscure and inferior quality—the type of Light which produces offspring that are inferior and corporeal.* What is brought to birth here results from the concealment of the Creator's perfect Countenance and Goodness. But when the mode of government springs from His love and His exaltedness, it means that the Creator, blessed be He, does not subject His supervision to the deeds of man, but rather employs His loftiness, which is exalted over all that pertains to the lower beings. It is a supervision which is independent of them. It is a tremendous and exalted radiation of Light which produces only Godly and sacred entities.

In the *Idra Zuta* of the *Zohar*, Z'O is called "Knowledge". It also calls him "first born son"—he who inherits the tokens (traits) of his father and mother. He is worthy of being considered their equal, for as the oldest son, who is in the image and form of his father, he is consulted by the latter in all matters.

The explanation of this matter runs as follows. Although matter must inevitably exist in it, in order for the mundane world to be in its proper state of

---

* TR. N. This government of Judgment rules because man's deeds are not in accord with Divine Will.

emendation, Light must so dominate over matter that its sanctification occurs immediately as a result. In this connection it is said in the Scriptures: "And it shall come to pass, that he that is left in Zion, and he that remaineth in Jerusalem, shall be called holy " . . . (Isaiah IV, 3).

The influence of the Light (brain) which Father and Mother impart to Z'O is increased in him to such an extent that he himself becomes a source for the world in its sanctified state. There is still material substance in that world, but the matter itself is sanctified.

However, in this process too there is a progression. Since the first condition of Z'O is not identical with that of Father and Mother, there are two states involved here. First, the state which prevails when Father and Mother send down a glow into Z'O, which fails, however, to elevate him to their own level. On the contrary, matter still has sway. But now some Light also is to be found in him. The second stage occurs when the Light dominates in Z'O, and the material part in him follows after it to the extent that the world becomes hallowed, as it will be in the future. This means that the light of Father and Mother has overpowered the essence in Z'O, so that he is now said to have assumed their traits.

When the Light of Father and Mother triumphs over the material substance of Z'O, he becomes their equal. With this intention, they themselves give him the "brain", which is a great and complete Light. However, if the intention is to leave Z'O in his inferior state—where only a glow is to be implanted in him—

then Father and Mother do not give the brain to Z'O. Only a little Light is transferred from their lowest degree, "Kingdom", otherwise known as Israel the Ancient, and Understanding. "Kingdom" effects this act in the role of Israel the Ancient, and Understanding by giving Z'O the brain. Hence he does not become equal of Father and Mother, for only when *they* impart the Light directly can he arrive at their status.

This is intimated in the word *Binah*, whose letters reveal that he (Z'O) is the son—*ben* of *Yud He'*. In the word *twunah* we find the two words *ben u-bat,* the "son and the daughter," as it is explained in the Idra Zuta.* For Binah (Intelligence) has the capacity to raise Z'O to a state which is equivalent to Father and Mother, but *Twunah* (Understanding) is the reverse for it imparts little Light.

When the world is governed in accordance with the first stage of maturity there *is* Light in the world, but not in sufficient quantity to sanctify all created beings.

However, when it is governed in accordance with the second stage of maturity then the Light is sufficiently ample to sanctify all creation.

Note that during the two thousand years of chaos, a supervision of immaturity reigned. Even the Law (Torah) was missing from the world. Man was totally sunk in matter. Of this period it is said in the Scriptures:

---

* TR. N. This designates a secondary degree of Light, issued not from Father and Mother themselves, but from their lower degrees.

". . . whose flesh is as the flesh of asses, and whose issue is like the issue of horses." (Ezekiel XXIII, 20). Therefore it is said of the Egyptian exile: "And they made their lives bitter . . . in mortar . . ." Exodus I, 14).* The patriarchs (Abraham, Isaac and Jacob) in their time began to improve conditions, but the task was only completed with the giving of the Law (Torah) on Sinai.

Truly speaking, during this present exile, the world is under the governing rule of the "infant Z'O" (while it partakes of nourishment from the Mother—*Binah*). This stage of infancy means that Z'O (lacking brain) possesses only the six *Sefirot* (dimensions), except during periods of prayer, when its Light is temporarily increased.

The Law (Torah) that exists in the world is the result of the three *Sefirot* "Mercy", "Power" and "Beauty", which are revealed when the infant Z'O is nourished. These Lights are called *Ruah*. They represent the actual degrees of the Torah that reside in "Beauty" (Z'O as a whole). Still lacking in the world, however, are the divine spirit, prophecy, and signs or miracles.

When, the Temple flourished, Z'O in its mature stages was the prevailing supervision. Then signs, miracles and prophecies abounded. These are all matters which come from the brains of Father and Mother, which are present in Z'O. It is a general rule that everything supernatural

---

* TR. N. "Mortar" here refers to the matter in which man was sunk. For further explanation see the *Zohar and Tikune Zohar*.

derives from that which is above the six *Sefirot* of Z'O
(namely, from the brain of Father and Mother—"Wisdom and Intelligence"). Yet even then the world was
not sanctified, for prophecy was the gift of only rare
individuals and the recognition of God only occurred by
virtue of signs and miracles.

However, in the days of Messiah the supervision will
emerge from Z'O's second stage of maturity. Of that
period it is said in the Scriptures: "And he that remaineth
in Jerusalem shall be called holy.' (Isaiah IV, 3.) For
great Light will envelop matter, to the extent that the
matter itself will be sanctified, and prophecy will spread
to all Israel, as it is said: ". . . I will pour out my Spirit
upon all flesh." (Joel III, 1.) Then wisdom will inhere
in all men as a natural trait, just as it is in the angels.
In the words of the prophet: "And they shall teach no
more every man his neighbor, and every man his brother,
saying Know the Lord . . ." (Jeremiah XXXI, 33.)

But until the second and most exalted stage of
maturity arrives, Z'O is not elevated, but is only taking
part in the process of becoming complete. For the
prenatal stage is the beginning of the structure: the stage
of infancy is his completion, and there are some matters
in Z'O which are only completed during the time he is
nourished. Maturity means the enlargement of all the
already constructed organs, so that they acquire the
necessary strength and power which belong to them.

Until Z'O reaches the second stage of maturity, the
Sefirot do not as yet possess all that belongs to them.
For since Z'O must acquire brain, he is not considered
complete until this brain dominates. But from the

second maturity onward, any further advance signifies actual elevations: Z'O's degrees are then transformed by ascents. From the time of Messiah on, the same condition leading from one elevation to another will be found in the stages of man.

However, the idea of "brain" exists as the dynamic power in every *Parezuf*. In fact, the power of each *Parezuf* is only as great as the measure of its brain.

But in Z'O whatever concerns the brain is subdivided further; that is, the process of joining the first three *Sefirot* (the brain) with the six following *Sefirot* (the six dimensions) is differentiated into particular stages.

However, in every instance the brain itself is a Light habiliment (garment) for the Line of Light from the Infinite, blessed be He. This Line of Light is changeless, no matter how far it extends. All the attributes receive it, enclothed in the brain. Individually, the attributes differ, and therefore the Line of Light within them differs, although in itself it remains changeless. This is in accord with the Creator's decree that the attributes should receive Lights appropriate for a supervision of reward and punishment, so that even the *functions* of the attributes themselves derive from the Line of Light.

The ultimate benefit of this motivation of the Sefirot of Z'O by the Line of Light, is that the Line of Light will eventually return the Impression to its own level thus rendering the government equal and unified.

Remember that the chief governing factor in the brain lies in "Knowledge" (Da'at—which is the soul of the attributes of Z'O). Therefore Z'O's attributes are manifest, while "Wisdom" and "Intelligence", the other elements of the brain, are not. The *Sefirot* "Wisdom" and "Intelligence" are the paths by which the attributes receive their "Knowledge" from the Line of Light "Knowledge" that is established to govern within the attributes according to this recipiency. (In other words, "Knowledge" is the governing factor in the brain of Z'O.)

The brain is different in each *Parezuf*, according to the Parezuf itself, and according to the period in which it is received. The power of the *Parezuf* and of its government depends upon its brain. But in Z'O the component parts are more distinctly segregated; the six lower *Sefirot*, as well as the three first *Sefirot* that comprise his brain, may actually be discerned in him.

Chapter Twenty-One

The Three Heads, The Beard and The Mazela

We have explained earlier, that the Creator's supervision by the measure of Judgment (Z'O) springs from love itself, as the Scriptures tell us: "But He that loves him chastens him betimes." (Prov. XIII, 24.) For when the son's conduct is unworthy, the father, out of love for his son, chastises him. On the other hand, when the son behaves well, he is endeared to the father. Because the Creator loves man, with His left hand He repels him and with His right He draws him nigh.

In love, two aspects may be discriminated: first, when the Creator is disposed toward bestowal of good, He continually tempers Judgment and even at times completely annuls it; and second, when chastisement, rooted in His very love, issues forth.

Note that *Arik* (Macroprosopus) represents only the Creator's love, and is emended solely in order to bestow goodness. The Cranium, the Brain and the other emendations which are found in its face are all degrees of mitigation for the Judgments of Z'O, tempering them and finally abolishing them altogether. These emendations are indicated by the Name 45.

When the Beard shines in ZO'N (Microprosopus and his "Kingdom", or feminine polarity) it means that the Creator's glory is manifest. Before this illumination, evil (the husk) is shamed and it dares no longer raise its head.

However, by reason of the fact that Judgment (Z'O) itself springs from Love and is rooted there, *Arik* himself is the source of Z'O. *Arik* therefore fixed with the emendation of three Heads and the Beard, which contain three *Havayas* and one which comprises them; these are the sources for "Mercy", "Judgment", and "Compassion"; and lastly, the vessel which receives them. (They correspond to the three pillars of Z'O and to his "Kingdom", the vessel of recipiency.) All are comprised in the *Mazela* (thirteenth emendation). Father and Mother, which are included in the *Mazela*, issue from it and are recognized as "Wisdom", "Intelligence" and "Knowledge".

From the foregoing we gain an insight into the evolution of the three pillars, namely: "Mercy", "Judgment" and "Compassion". Actually, they represent one collective Light that is issued from *Arik,* the upper source. The whole of "Mercy", "Judgment" and "Compassion" were originally inherent in the Concealed Wisdom, or the third Head, and they correspond to its Y'H'W. The light is designated the "Crystal Dew". But in the third head it is nothing but a collective Light which remains unmanifest.

However, when the Beard issues from Concealed Wisdom, the three pillars of "Mercy", "Judgment" and "Compassion" become more manifest and are ready to

evolve and extend to their proper place.   Thus we find
that Concealed Wisdom veils, while the Beard unveils—
and fashions all the progressive degrees of evolution up
to Z'O.

In connection with these three Heads there are
profound secrets relating to the upper source (where all
is equal) and the issuance of the diversified paths of justice (Z'O).   In *Arik* there is no diversity whatever;
there is no right, no left, and no center.   But from him
emanate the right, the left and the center pillars, and in
this act of emanation there are exceedingly concealed
secrets.   All are comprised in these three Heads, for they
are the source of the right, left, and center pillars which
issue downward from them.

Arik is still exclusively right and he is that *Parezuf*
whose function is to bestow the all-inclusive Good of the
upper unity; yet below him, the paths begin to be diversified. Here Father becomes the right, and Mother the left.
So much more apparent is the division between the many
paths of right and left which follow from Father and
Mother down.

So that they may extend further, the Beard serves
to issue and make more manifest the three pillars of
"Mercy", "Judgment" and "Compassion", which were
hidden in the Concealed Wisdom.

Father and Mother ("Wisdom" and "Intelligence")
administer guidance to Judgment (Z'O) to the end that
he may be firmly established.   They are a composite of
all the sources of and reasons for the Judgments which it
is necessary to establish.   In other words, in them is contained the answer to what type of guidance is necessary
in order to properly establish Z'O.

"Wisdom" fulfills the name it bears, since it carries out the general guidance of Z'O. "Intelligence" also fulfills the implication of its name by providing a specific surveillance. These two together, "Wisdom" and "Intelligence", constantly observe the world and maintain the perpetual existence of justice (Z'O).

Evidently, since "Crown" (*Arik Anpin*) represents the bestowal of good on the part of the Supreme Will, whereas the Judgments of Z'O suit the merits of the nether beings, a great deal of guidance is necessary in order to insure the proper supervision.

"Wisdom" and "Intelligence" are attributes of guidance. It is through them that justice (Z'O) is established. They constantly insure that their union shall be continuous, for it is by this perpetual union of Father and Mother that the worlds are maintained. Their function is also to bestow, whenever necessary, new power and additional elevation for establishing "Kingdom". This is achieved through periodic unions, for the purpose of adding new "brain".

Chapter Twenty-Two

Feminine Polarity of Z'O

This *Sefira*—"Kingdom"—is the power of the existing emendations in that all the nine *Sefirot* constitute the collective bounty which the Creator bestows on the world. These nine *Sefirot* effect all the divine occurrences in the world. But the feminine polarity of Z'O is the general container of the existing emendations (vessels) which receives the substance of those occurrences. Thus it is within her that all diversities and changes in conditions of being take place according to the different bestowals for these occurrences. The sum total of her ascents and descents, as well as her many other conditions, manifest as the general and diversified conditions affecting the existence of the nether beings.

The most important nether beings are the children of Israel. Thus the feminine polarity is the true source of everything that concerns Israel, and after Israel, of everything concerning the rest of created beings who are guided after them.

Chapter Twenty-Three

A Virtuous Woman is a Crown to Her Husband

(Proverbs XII, 4)

The feminine polarity is but a single point; the nine *Sefirot* which she acquires are considered to be supplemental. "Kingdom" (the feminine polarity) is the actual source for the nether beings. She alone makes room for darkness and the actual existence of evil in the government. The vacuum is never due to the intention of the Bestower, but is the result of the iniquity of the recipient. Nevertheless, as far as "Kingdom" is concerned, the vacuum, or flaw which permits the existence of evil has two meanings: on the one hand, it debases her, and on the other, it elevates her, since all of this has been instituted for no other purpose than to disclose the upper unity, and no glory of the Creator is disclosed except through "Kingdom".* It is for this reason that the Creator fashioned "Kingdom" with an innate lack

---

* TR. N. Since Kingdom possesses evil and darkness, which is utterly opposed to the unity of the Creator, when unity is disclosed through her it means that even these extreme forces of opposition to unity are subdued and forced to admit the unity of the Supreme Being.

and obscurity which put her in need of extensive emendations, whereas the bestower (in this case Z'O) who, on
his own part, lacks nothing, requires no such emendations.

When "Kingdom", having been emended, is completely perfect she emerges from the evil, transforming it
to good. Then praise for "Kingdom" rises to the Infinite
Itself, for the Glory of the Creator is exalted through
her, and she is called the "crown of her husband." Because the Creator, blessed be He, desired that this source
to the nether beings should achieve this elevated goal, He
made her incomplete. Moreover, He caused her to be
dependent upon man's deeds, for receiving her full
measure of Light. In this way, only a small portion of
the bounty that is rightly hers is settled in her, while the
balance remains with the bestower above her. For if the
nether beings merit the bestowal of bounty they will
receive their additional Light (that which was withheld
from "Kingdom") and their worth will be infinitely
exalted. If, on the other hand, the nether beings are
not meritorious, they continue to remain at their inferior
stage.

If, from the first, the nether beings had not been
subjected to evil and therefore crowned with all their
Lights, the emendation which must be effected in "Kingdom" would never have been accomplished. To accom-
modate man's prerequisite, "Kingdom" forms only a
single source point and an exceedingly small Light which
is supplemented and rounded out by the nine *Sefirot*.
When man increases in merit, not only does "Kingdom"
increase her power, but also Z'O, the bestower which is
above "Kingdom". Thus it is said: "Give ye strength

unto God." (Psalms LXVIII, 35). This signifies only
that man is the cause for the additional blessing and
increase of power originating in the bestower.

The bounty here referred to is the brain acquired
by Z'O; at times it departs from him and at other times
it returns. But the nether beings lack that essence of
Light which is necessary for their construction, and for
that reason "Kingdom" is no more that one point. Moreover, in Z'O this causes only a departure of Light, whereas in "Kingdom" it results in destruction of the entire
edifice. In the case of the bestower only the bounty is
withheld whereas the nether beings are actually ruined.
This is what is meant when we speak of "the descent of
the nine *Sefirot* of 'Kingdom' to the shells." The feminine
polarity ("Kingdom") has its source in the *Sefirot* of
"Knowledge", "Beauty" and "Foundation" (The middle
pillar) and is bound with them throughout the gestation, infancy and maturity of Z'O.

The Creator's goal is conveyed in the verse from the
Psalms, for it is written: "Your wonderful works which
you have done and your thoughts which are toward
us . . ." (Psalm XL, 6). For the whole arrangement of
His bestowals is intended exclusively for the nether
beings. Yet whatever is bestowed is contained within
fixed limits and measures, according to man's needs.

Thus, with every order of Light which is arranged
in Z'O, whether it be that of the three lower *Sefirot*—
"Triumph", "Glory" and "Foundation", which designates
Z'O's external *Parezuf* in the stage of gestation—or that
of "Mercy", "Judgment" and "Beauty" which is the
middle *Parezuf* (the stage of nourishment), or that of

"Wisdom", "Intelligence" and "Knowledge", which is the internal *Parezuf* (the stage of maturity), "Kingdom" must necessarily be bound, for she complements and completes Z'O, and all these Lights she requires for her existence, are intended for her benefit. Therefore the union of this feminine polarity with Z'O must be perpetual; every thought of bestowal is intended for her alone so that she may transmit this Light to Israel.

Chapter Twenty-Four

Back to Back: Face to Face: and The Process of Sawing Through

The degrees of either proximity or distance which exists between the world of created beings and the Supreme Bestower is designated as either "back" (*ahuraim*) or "face" (*ponim*) of the Bestower. When the illumination emanates from the back, it means that the nether beings are at a distance from the Bestower. It is as though a man turns away from his friend; he turns his back on him. When the illumination issues from the face, it indicates the closeness of the bestower to the recipient.

Those Lights and bestowals in which no "cheerful countenance" is apparent denote departure and remoteness, and correspond to the "back". Those Lights and bestowals exhibiting benevolence, a cheerful countenance, and proximity, are termed "face". Thus, wherever there is extreme remoteness between one *Parezuf* and another it denotes a condition of "back to back"; whereever there is extreme proximity of *Parezufim* it indicates a condition of "face to face'. For in "back to back' a particular *Parezuf* turns his face to one side, and another turns his face to the other side. They are turned around

244

and do not face each other at all, each facing in an opposite direction. The "face to face" situation is just the reverse. Here, the *Parezufim* turn full face toward each other, in complete unity. The middle point between these two extremes is termed either "face to back" or "back to face" in that one turns his face toward the other, though the latter is turned aside.

Note that the created beings in their perfect state approach the Creator with intimate hearts—as a wife her husband—and He turns to them with love. Such a condition exists when the feminine polarity stands face to face with Z'O.

But when they are in an imperfect state, they stand back to back with their Creator, and dare not raise their heads before Him. While He, in turn, withholds His love from them.

Israel emerges from the very womb of the Creator and is united with Him, for it, like the soul, is a part of God. In this respect there is never, in all eternity, any separation. Therefore, even when the feminine polarity stands back to back with Z'O, there is but one body for both. An inherent bond exists between the upper divinity, which comprises all the aggregate Lights, and the souls of Israel. Hence, there is no separation between them. At those times when Israel lacks completion the Creator only tolerates them, without turning His great love toward them; then Israel lacks the temerity to face Him.

Even prior to the descent of the souls to the mundane plane, their very being is sustained by the Creator; they are in no way separate from Him, and they rejoice

in His Light. Moreover, they have no power but that
which they derive from Him. In that condition, however, they experience the embarrassment of one who
"eats unearned bread." Such a state implies that the
feminine polarity mentioned earlier stands back to back
with Z'O and that whatever power she has is derived
from Z'O alone.

A similar condition of embarrassment at receiving
without having earned governs all other created beings,
including the angels, because they execute their functions
involuntarily and have no self-imposed task. That is,
they perform no duty outside of that which they receive
from the upper Source.*

However, the Creator, blessed be He, desired that
man be responsible for at least one specific form of service not under the Heavenly jurisdiction. This required
that the Supreme Will assign to man the kind of task
which he could fulfill without requiring aid from the
Creator Himself—as he does in all other matters. Here
it would be necessary for man to act of his own accord;
and so God provided the process in which Mother ("Intelligence") abandoned Z'O and entered "Kingdom".
This act separating "Kingdom" from Z'O is called "sawing". By "sawing herself off from him", Mother enters

---

* TR. N. Their specific tasks are assigned to them, for as
the sages teach, an angel is capable of fulfilling only a single type
of action. For example, the angels who came to Abraham each
had his own assignment: one was to destroy Sodom; one to inform
Sarah; one to heal Abraham. No one angel could perform all three
tasks alone.

into "Kingdom" directly, and constructs it herself, without the benefit of Z'O. This process provides the source of the nether beings ("Kingdom") with a power which eliminates their dependence on the Upper Light, a power enabling them to act by their own choice and not by compulsion. This free will provides man with the opportunity to acquire merit and to become glorified, as it falls to man alone to appear before the King.

In relation to the Creator, man is like a wife to her husband. In such a relationship, the King turns to man with love, for man's virtue or merit is of a different degree from that of all other created beings. Man's service is the result of his own choice. It is this factor of choice which brings greater advantage to creation, resulting in its perfection and completion. Consequently, man is partner to the Creator in maintaining and perfecting His world.

Chapter Twenty-Five

Mercies and Judgements of Knowledge

The "Mercies" and "Judgments" of the *Sefira* "Knowledge" are divided between Z'O and his feminine polarity. The "Mercies" are given to Z'O and the Judgments relegated to the feminine polarity. What follows is an explanation of the terms M'D and M'N. In either case, *Mem* stands for water, or bestowal; the letter *Dalet* in M'D qualifies it as musculine, while the letter *Nun* in M'N is feminine.

Note that *Nukbah*, the feminine polarity, is merely one-tenth of Z'O, which is made up of nine *Sefirot*. Z'O represents the bestower and *Nukbah* is the recipient. They are respectively like the heavens which are high above, and the earth which lies spread below; the implication being that the bestower is very high above the recipient.

Nevertheless, in their governing roles, they are equally balanced: the entire government of the right pillar is assigned to Z'O, and the entire government of the left is assigned to the feminine polarity.

Recall, however, that the chief governing power in a *Parezuf* lies in its "Knowledge" (*Da'at*); so that "Knowledge" is divided between Z'O and the feminine polarity in order for them to rule equally. This "partner-ship" between "Mercy" and "Judgment" is the very essence of the government of the world. The means to the perfection of creation, it was divided equally by the Creator between Himself and man, making them partners. That is why the Creator stands ready to emend all that concerns the bestowal which relates to the right pillar, as it is written: ". . . My right hand hath spanned the heavens", while the nether beings are responsible for emending all that concerns the recipiency which relates to the left pillar, as it is said: "Mine hand also hath laid the foundation of the earth." (Isaiah XLVIII, 14).

In the *Midrash* there is a comment on the words from the Song of Songs: "Undefiled is my dove" (*tamoti*-my dove).* The word *tamoti*, according to the sages, resembles *taomoti* which means "my twin sister", and the idea is that God proclaims "Not that I am greater than she, nor that she is greater than I," but that they actually stand equal.

Although the distance between God and ourselves is very great, He granted us this equality. This is the idea behind the tenth position of the feminine polarity, which is nevertheless capable of being the recipient for all of Z'O.

The partnership that exists between Israel and the Creator is as described in the following: The Creator devised the darkness inherent in man as a means for main-taining the evil which is to be transmuted into good. Because of this man must effect many emendations in

---

* TR. N. "My dove" stands for the congregation of Israel.

this darkness. On His part, the Creator grants fresh
bestowals to man in acordance with the degree of emendation which he has effected commensurate with his own
preparations. These bestowals correspond to the aggregation of "Mercies" and "Judgments" of the *Sefira*
"Knowledge"; They are the Names 45 and 52 as well
as M'D and M'N. M'N therefore consists of the new
Lights which derive from the contents of the Name 52.
They are extracted from all the Primordial Kings, and
from the newly emended parts that belong to the Name
52. This is the sum total of darkness inherent in man
which must be selected from evil and transformed into
good. New bestowals of divine Light descend according
to the selections which rise from the Name 52. They
are the M'D (or bestowal) of the Name 45.

Following the fall of the first man (Adam) all of
the other major transgressions that succeeded him, sparks
descended into the shells. This accumulation of sparks is
added to those that still remain as a result of the shattering of the vessels, thus making it necessary to extract
these as well, for it is from them that the New M'N and
M'D are to issue.

To clarify this still further we must reiterate that
"Kingdom" is the source of the nether beings. She is
also the dominating factor of the divine holiness, and the
word "Kingdom" bears out the connotation of reign or
dominion. But her "other side" (sitra ahara) has no
dominion whatsoever; for dominion belongs to the
Creator, blessed be He. He created, and He holds sway
over His creation. What then remains for the "other
side" to dominate? There are instances in which the

Creator desires to grant rulership to the "other side", despite the fact that this rule is not her due. The Talmud cites such an instance in the case of Israel's exile, for then the Jews were deprived of their glory, which was given instead to the nations of the world.

Thus we find that portions of "Kingdom" itself are, so to speak, enclothed in the shells, which are evil, in that a portion of the upper dominion is given over to the "other side" (*sitra ahara*). But this is only a small portion of dominion—no more than what is stipulated by the Upper Degree—and actually nothing more than her sparks. Evil reigns in the world because the "other side" already acquired adequate sustenance and rulership with the shattering of the vessels. It will therefore avoid being totally eradicated until the sparks from the Primordial Kings are entirely selected. Moreover, further power is granted to the "other side" with the continuation of man's iniquities, reflections of the M'N of "Kingdom", which fell into the shells. Yet everything pertaining to "Kingdom" is tempered by the souls of men, which descend into the shells, bearing an actual portion of her within themselves.

The lack of emendation, or adequate preparation in the whole of creation is in the exact measure of dominion that is granted the "other side".

Emendations and adequate preparations are supplemented to creation to the extent that the evil inclination is deprived of its power. In this case the Creator, blessed be He, increases the bestowal of the Divine Light to creation.

This is the general procedure depicting the selection of M'N and Sparks, to which the descent of M'D corresponds.

Man's present task is still to emend that which is corrupt, and to restore that which is lost. When this is accomplished, "new M'N" appears, for these letters represent added efforts at preparation and increasing ascent in the general nature of the nether beings who are normally rooted in the Name 52. "Kingdom" raises all this, while M'D, the new bestowals, descend toward the renewed preparations.

Chapter Twenty-Six

The First and Second Unions

Despite the fact that man's worship is not under the jurisdiction of Heaven, he could accomplish nothing without the will of the King.* For it is the Creator who gives man the very power to act and to render service. This refers to what we are told by the sages, namely that it is more difficult to fulfill a precept which is commanded than one which is not commanded: while he who assumes an obligation without being commanded, is called ignorant.

This is the power which was given generally to all of Israel on Mount Sinai and which is renewed for each man every day. It is this that constitutes the first union between Z'O and "Kingdom" by fashioning the vessel and thereby conferring power upon the feminine polarity ("Kingdom") to enable her to perform her part: that is, raising M'N from the Name 52. After that, the second,

---

* TR. N. That is, man of his own free will must choose whether to assume the yoke of worship and service or to remain unconcerned about fulfilling the Law and commandments.

all-important union with Z'O, whose purpose is to bring forth fruit, takes place.**

** TR. N.   These same two unions occur also in man through his worship.   For the Torah commands "cleave to your God"— and since the chasm between man and God is due to the darkness and evil inherent in man, the first step towards fulfillment of his command is service (*abodah*), by which evil is obliterated. This is the first union which gives man the power to become a perfect vessel.   When he achieves total purification and becomes this complete vessel, he is then able to unit with God for eternity and thereby fulfills the precept urging him to "cleave to your God".   This is the second union, whereby the fruits that man enjoys are the glorious revelations of his own soul.

Chapter Twenty-Seven

The Two Types of Unions

There are unions that take place by means of kissing, while others are accomplished through the medium of the "Foundation". "Kissing" serves the purpose of complete unity, while the union of the "Foundations" exists for the purpose of producing fruit. It is the former type of union that is referred to when we say that the Creator conjoined Israel to Himself: this is the actual meaning of the words: "Let Him kiss me with the kisses of His mouth." (Song of Solomon I, 2). Because of this great union, Israel is able to execute its emendations, for at the outset it is necessary that the people bind themselves with the upper Lights in a total and mutual bond, as a result of which they are enabled to perform their emendations, and consequently to increase the sanctity and the upper Light—the very fruits of the union itself.

This process is engendered by the great love which the Creator arouses in Israel, and which, in turn, promotes His desire for their worship.

Chapter Twenty-Eight

The Two Feminine Polarities: Leah and Rachel*

There are two sources for the nation of Israel. The first is the general source for the entire nation, both good and bad: it is rooted higher up amongst the sources of the upper Lights, which are fashioned specifically for the purpose of evolving Israel. Nevertheless, the principal government does not depend on these Lights, and so, although it is an exalted one, there are not many offspring from this source.

However, there is another source for Israel, which corresponds to its deeds. This one is subject to the many changing conditions which occur in the congregation; therefore it produces numerous offspring. All the new occurrences which take place in the supervision, whether they be for good, or evil, are dependent on this source. We designate the two sources as "Leah" and "Rachel".

Composed of the *Sefira* "Kingdom" within the *Parezuf* mother (Intelligence), Leah is the origin of

---

* TR. N. "Leah" and "Rachel" correspond to the two "King-dom's" (feminine counterparts) of Z'O.

Israel, and she is most exalted. She occupies the place of the brain and is not subject to such changes as take place in Rachel. With her, union is not of chief importance. On the contrary, she is representative of the concealed world.

But Rachel is a source for man according to his deeds. Her conditions are constantly changing along with the changing degrees of virtue in man. The principal government depends on her for she is the "mistress of the house." The principal union takes place with her, because only Rachel can produce a renewal of bounty. Most important of all is the union of the *Parezuf* Israel with Rachel.* However, the completion of all aspects of bestowal is achieved through the other unions which take place throughout the day, that is, the unions with Leah.

---

* TR. N. Z'O bears the two names "Jacob" and "Israel". In its highest aspect it is "Israel".

Chapter Twenty-Nine

The Worlds of Creation, Formation and Action

"Kingdom" (of the world of Emanation) is the source for the worlds of "Creation", "Formation" and "Action", as well as for the nether beings that reside in them. Everything that is to eventually take place in them must first be found as a root in "Kingdom". The manner in which the contents of the source are issued from "Kingdom" to the nether beings resembles that of the *Nefesh* (the soul) which is related to all the motions of the body. Another important aspect of this relationship is *how* the soul functions in the body; how it is established in it, and how its force circulates therein.

"Kingdom" unites with her branches in B'Y'A, that is in the worlds of "Creation", "Formation" and "Action". In these there may be found both Godliness and severed beings, which is not the same as in the world of Emanation, for there are to be found only the Lights of divinity. With respect to her descent for the purpose of uniting with her branches, "Kingdom" is called "the Glory of the Throne." While all the paths by which the branches unite with her are recognized in the paths of these worlds, or in that which pertains to their palaces. Thus each palace has an individual *Nefesh*. Next to that there is one *Ruah* (the next higher degree of Spirit) for all its palaces and each single *Ruah* lodging there, unites with all the others to become one collective *Ruah*. They are nonetheless still considered to be severed beings. There is only one *Neshama* (soul—the next degree beyond *Ruah*) for all; here are included all the Godly *Sefirot* of B'Y'A ("Creation", "Formation" and "Action").

In the beginning this *Neshama* brings *Ruah* to birth. *Ruah* then travels until it reaches the palace specifically designed for it, and once there, rules all the other entities contained in that world. This procedure occurs principally in the world of "Creation", but through evolution, *Ruah* is drawn even to the worlds of "Formation" and "Action".

In that palace which is designated "the Holy of Holies" (the first three *Sefirot* in the world of "Creation") the Glory of complete perfection of the worlds abides continually. Her presence required there in order for the branches to unite themselves with her. This procedure takes place only in the world of "Emanation" so that the Glory (i.e. "Kingdom") may function as a collective power for the other worlds, gathering their intended bestowel unto itself. In the world of "Emanation", "Kingdom" is represented as the feminine counterpart of Z'O. Note that before she can be considered as a collective power in order to extend bounty to the collectivity of branches, she must, in fact comprise all the branches. This requires that all the worlds be comprised within each other, so that they may all be bound in the palace of the Holy of Holies. Thereafter all rise to the world of "Emanation", where they receive energy from their source—"Kingdom". Here she is considered a collective power, which enables her to unite and thus draw bounty. This connotes the construction of the feminine polarity in the world of "Emanation", since all the nether worlds that have been included within each other reside there.

All of the foregoing relates to the angels, which are the servants of the worlds, and the hosts of "Kingdom".

Recall that the M'N, on the other hand, is a more detailed emendation which is produced by the new bestowal for the purpose of bringing creation to completion. The function of raising M'N does not pertain to the angels, but to Israel alone. It pertains to the souls of the Zadikim (the righteous, who produce M'N) by virtue of their good deeds.

All that we have learned up to this point relates to the aggregate Parezufim of the world of "Emanation", which are arranged into a government of reward and punishment; however, the occult government, upon which revolves the emendation of the worlds, is beyond this supervision.

Chapter Thirty

The Uniting of the Names 45 and 52

The *Parezufim* of the world of Emanation are fashioned from the union of the two Names, 45 and 52. The secret here is that the Creator, blessed be He, uncovered the darkness which he had invented by concealing His Countenance, the act responsible for all evil in the world. All this He devised within set laws and boundaries, as He desired. He therefore knows these limits and is also aware of what is necessary in order to emend the situation for the purification of the world and for the establishment of a supervision that is absolute free from evil.

All the darkness and corruption that evil incurs has its source in the Name 52, while all the emendations have their source in the Name 45. It is necessary to reveal a type of nether being that would correspond to the various corruptions which are rooted in the Name 52.

The Creator effected all the unions between the two Names 45 and 52 for He knew that these were necessary to correct the existing darkness. To the Creator alone it is apparent that there are matters in the essence of creation whose emendation depends on increase of Light and goodness; and that these are other matters in the

essence of creation, whose emendation depends on trials
and poverty, and concealment of Light, and that this is
not dependent on merit or demerit, but rather on the
change which the Creator made in the essence of the
bounty for creation. Whatever the Creator does is certainly for the good. Therefore, both the abundant bestowal which He makes, as well as impoverishment and
concealment of Light, are certainly aimed at the single
goal of executing emendations in the world.

There are some emendations which can only be produced through negative means and there are some which
can only be produced through grace. It only depends
on the essence of creation itself. All these matters, in
fact, depend on the unions of the Names 45 and 52,
because varying results are drawn from them. Thus,
there are unions which result in much good, and there
are those which result in concealment. The function of
the Name 45, for example, is to emend M'N, but this
emendation coresponds to pre-existing necessities.

There are different kinds of M'N (half masculine,
half feminine *Parezuf*) to be raised by the different souls.
But, the source for the subdivisions of the souls is profound and concealed; it is unknown, for in order to
know it would be necessary to know all the *Sefirot,* and
this knowledge rests with the Creator alone. To man it
remains imperceptible. However this we *do* know, that
the emendation of creation is apportioned among the
souls; that to each and every one the Upper Wisdom
allotted a suitable portion. The difference between them
reflects the varying conditions of the world. Remember
that one soul will be emended by means of abundance of

good, while another will be allotted a task of emendation
by way of poverty and tribulations. However, when
the Creator desires to supervise the world in this way (i.e.
in accord with the need of creation), He allots to each soul
a portion of the task. In some cases it is to be achieved
by means of abundance of Light, in others by means of
deprivation of Light. This is evidently not at all parallel
to their deeds. Nevertheless, it is this form of government that presides in the world at present. Whereas in
the world to come each receives according to his deeds.
Yet here, where emendations must be executed, the means
employed—whether harsh or gentle—depend on chance.
Should God determine to govern the world only according to the deeds of mankind, then he resorts to a system
of reward and punishment of the type that resides in
the *Parezufim* of the world of Emanation.

Note that at times the righteous souls, like the
wicked ones, experience evil in order to purge creation
through their own trials and their own purification.
However, great indeed is the power of the souls who
emend in this way, for all that befalls them is not according to their deeds, but according to the existing
supervision which is fixed in the whole occult government. Therefore the reward due them is not only a
bestowal of good, for emending the general existing supervision merits a doubled and redoubled reward: but by
virtue of their meritorious deeds, through which they
have caused emendation of the general supervision, they
have benefitted the whole world.

However the Creator does not always employ supervision by decree. At times He employs the supervision

of reward and punishment instead. The chance method mentioned previously is known as "Mazel", which comes as a decree and not according to the deeds of man. Thus, when the Creator knows that there exists men of valor and fortitude, capable of bearing the necessary trials, He employs this administration. This is what is conveyed in the words: "The Lord tries the righteous." (Psalms XI, 5). Toward the end of the exile the Creator will employ mostly this method, for the intention then will be to effect a general emendation of the entire world.

Therefore it will be necessary to govern according to the supervision of unity (by decree) for from a great concealment is born an equally great revelation, through which perfection will be granted to the world. Thus we find that even the manifestation of unity will come as a well-earned reward and not as an act of grace, although the sinner will enjoy this revelation without having labored for it. As it is expressed in the Scriptures: ". . . For I will pardon them whom I reserve." (Jeremiah L, 20). Then even the benefit enjoyed by the sinners will be due to the reward of the righteous who have suffered trials on behalf of the general supervision. For the righteous themselves there will be additional reward, since they will motivate Judgment itself to sanction the bestowal of good upon the wicked. And in this, too, lies reward for the righteous. Generally speaking, the righteous merit the revelation of the Heavenly Good in order that they may complete certain portions in creation.

We see then that the Creator makes use of the supervision which He knows will benefit His world. At that period when He employs the government of "Mazel", it is for the purpose of benefitting the entire creation. There is no need for this government to function continuously, but only in those periods when the Creator stipulates it out of recognized necessity.

The present supervision is composed of twenty-eight different cycles. The source of the supervision of the nether beings of Kingdom, is a supervision of good and evil which is implanted in them. The various incidents affecting man depend on these rotating cycles, and not on the deeds of the nether beings. This is signified in the words of the sages: "He is righteous yet he suffers trials and tribulations; he is wicked yet he enjoys good fortune." But even Moses himself did not possess the knowledge concerning which righteous man shall experience good, and which trouble. Such knowledge would entail an understanding of the reasons governing the specific apportionment of the task of emendation between the different souls, and those reasons are hidden from us. Indeed, the supervision of *Mazel* does not always prevail; only the Creator Himself knows when to employ it and when to use the principle of reward and punishment.

Moreover, the Creator desired to combine these two types of supervision. To this end He causes even what issues according to Higher Law (decree) to appear to man as punishment for some misdeed, as though man himself had brought on all that was in fact decreed for him. Such was the case of the suffering of that saintly Rebi Hakadosh, who arranged the Mishneh. His suffering (at a certain period of his life) came as the result of a specific act, and likewise the surcease of suffering was also due to a specific act. Kabbalistic literature claims, however, that the suffering was decreed to him, and was not the result of his act, although it appeared to be so.

In the main, the government of the world does revolve upon the axis of the essence of beings themselves, and it is in accord with thier inherent defects, that an emendation is prepared for them. But until the time when the Creator will produce the final means for bringing everything to completion, He has fixed the government of reward and punishment to serve in the world. He arranged this order so that it should not deviate from the center of the profound upper supervision, which works by absolute decree. On the contrary, everything that pertains to the upper supervision is combined with everything that pertains to the supervision of reward and punishment. But neither the upper government, nor its connction with reward and punishment, is clearly known to any prophet or seer, since this knowledge rests only with the Creator Himself.

However, man's ignorance of the workings of the supervision is due to its inception in *RDL'Y* (*Raisha D'Lo Yawda*) (the Unknown Head). In other words, the first union, by means of which the Names 45 and 52 were joined, took place in the Unknown Head, bringing all the subsequent unions in the world of Emanation in accord with itself. Thus, all that pertains to the union in the Unknown Head is unmanifest and unperceived, so that the government immanent in it is equally veiled. These combinations are called the "uncertainties" of the Unknown Head. The unions of the Names 45 and 52 were effected within the *Sefira* "Kingdom" of the Infinite. So, too were all the other unions required for the purpose of ultimately achieving the complete emendation. All was consummated in this unfathomable "Kingdom". But the actual revelation of the unions of 45 and 52— according to the superior government of decree (*Mazel*) —as well as its union and combination with the government of reward and punishment, is arranged in this world known as *RDL'Y*.

Here, all these unions are present to the extent that it becomes impossible to judge from which of their constituent parts she is built, or by which of the supervisions she governs. All the upper decrees of the government of *Mazel,* which are newly issued, spring from this Head, but its path is utterly inexplicable. Everything in this realm remains "uncertain" and unclarified. Were we but to know this Head, then we would inevitably perceive the edifice of the whole of the world of Emanation which follows it. As a consequence, we would know the truth of the government of *Mazel* and all its fixed statutes. But since this Head is unknown to us, we truly do not know the source of all these things—and many varying interpretations can be placed upon one and the same aspect of things. This is borne out in the Biblical words of Exodus 33, verse 19, expressed as a decree known to the Creator alone: ". . . and (I) will be gracious to whom I will be gracious, and will show mercy on whom I will show Mercy."

However, this Unknown Head fulfills still another function. Man's actions effect emendations in creation, according to the Creator's pre-arranged will. As we stated previously, He left certain things for man to emend, and it is in this process that His eternal reward

to man is based.   This means that the Creator must first
judge the exact nature of the act, and then fix the reward. We must remember that there is no forgetfulness
in Him; when He judges each particular act, it is with
due consideration of the past, the present and the future.
For an act of reparation following one misdeed is neither
equivalent to an act of reparation following two misdeed, nor to two acts of reparation following one misdeed, and so on, in the endless chain of relationships
possible between misdeeds and reparation.

The Creator sees everything. He judges the deed in
relation to the whole, and thus appoints the final reward.
All of this will be made clear to the eyes of all created
beings in the great Day of Judgment, when they finally
become aware of the Creator's righteous judgment.

It is the Unknown Head, which is engraved with
the sum total of knowledge pertaining to the supervision
of reward and punishment.   Also here, through the
unions of the Names 45 and 52, the Creator judges each
and every act.   This situation gives constant power to
all the unions because every act, whether small or great,
is judged in relation to the whole.   Thus, everything
pertaining to the government of the world of man lodges
in the Unknown Head.

Chapter Thirty-One

The Elevation Attained Through Sabbath

When we speak of the immaturity or the maturity of Z'O, the main point relates to the governing of the world. In other words, Z'O's condition is to effect both mature and immature actions on this plane. To illustrate: at the time of exile, the world is governed from the mature stage of Z'O, according to that period when he is nourished by his Mother, while at the time of redemption, the world will be supervised by Z'O in a mature condition. A perfect government will issue from him.

But the prevalence of immaturity or maturity, or elevations on particular days (even at the present time) does not indicate that the world has reached a superior form of government. If that truly were the case, the entire condition of the world would be altered. The fact is that although the elevation wrought in these periods rules over all the particulars concerned, it is still not in complete dominion, but develops rather to meet the occasion. Similarly, the stars rule according to the different hours of the day and night, while the particular bounty which they bestow at all times is only received by that which is immediately subject to them; yet all creation is benefitted by this type of rule. This special bestowal does not actually change the conditions of existence, although it brings greater elevation and establishes a certain degree of sanctity during the reign.

The same principle applies where prayers effect a rule of either immaturity or maturity, for these are nothing but intermitent emendations. They are incapable of establishing a lasting government of maturity. However even these temporary emendations are necessary for the daily renewal of bounty, and when this act is accomplished Z'O reverts to its normal stage of govrnment. However, when the heavenly government will be established in actual maturity, Israel will be redeemed.

Chapter Thirty-Two

Prophetic Visions

The Creator exhibits His Light to His seers through prophetic images which reveal to them a limited extent of His attributes and government. Manifold phases, for example, are disclosed through manifold images. The Midrash conveys something of this idea in the following excerpt:

> " 'Face to face' (an expression in the Bible) refers to the Israelites who stood face to face with God at Mount Sinai. From this expression we learn that He showed them a cheerful face, a laughing face."

All of this must nonetheless be apprehended in terms of metaphor; to cite such an instance—in the Kabbalah there are the circles, and there is the line. When the Creator portrays to the prophet the evolution of powers which maintain this world—for every superior power supports one that is inferior to it—He shows circles within circles, with the mundane world at the center. When He desires to show the attributes in their role as governing factors, that is, as right, left, and center pillars, He displays the entire content of the vertical line, which is subdivided into "Mercy", "Judgment" and "Compassion", in the image of a man's body and all that is encompassed within it.   When He shows either those attributes that are closer to His own perfection, or those that are remoter, He shows them respectively, as internal or external forms.

If, on the other hand, the Creator desires to make known all these attributes, He displays all these images at once, and though they may seem contradictory to each other, it does not matter, since the overall intention is to instruct the seer in whatever part of the attributes his particular vision can comprehend.

"Kingdom" is called the "image of God", for she is the source of the images (mental visions) of all created beings which are the branches of the upper attributes.   It is actually a replica of the Creator's government and attributes that she provides in the visions of the prophets.

The prophets conceive of the upper Lights only by means of their translation into the images which they perceive.   This enables them to grasp only "Kingdom", from which they may increase in all wisdom and so finally perceive the upper Lights.   This is often explained in the *Zohar* and particularly in the *Zohar* on Emendations. It is what the prophet Jeremiah meant when he said: "But let him that glorieth glory in this, that he understandeth and knoweth me . . ." (Jeremiah IX, 23)* and "Kingdom" our world is the gate of God.

_____

* TR. N.   The word "this" refers to "Kingdom".

According to the Kabbalah the universe resides in a system where an effect is a result of a cause which is indirect, but is neither random nor accidental. The root of this causality is imbedded in the creation and constitutes a passage to the physical realm. Within the chain of "cause and effect" is found the life of man, and everything which happens in it. If man will see and understand this chain, he will know how to direct his life towards his goal through the easiest and best path, and will know to implement in a balanced way the love of his fellowman, as it is written, "Love your fellowman as yourself".

"...and after forty days that the column will rise from the earth to the heavens in front of the eyes of the whole world the Mashiach will be revealed. From the East side a star will shine in surround this star and will make war with it from all the sides, three times a day for seventy days. And all the people of the world will see..." (Zohar, 'Shemot' part 101).

THE WISDOM OF KABBALAH AND THE AGE OF AQUARIUS

The wisdom of Kabbalah dates from thousands of years ago and has accompanied the world since its creation. The sages of Kabbalah have used its hidden knowledge in order to analyze and understand the reason for the universe and the reason for life. Today, in the age of Aquarius, the age of revelations and discoveries, this wisdom is being revealed to the public at large. The wisdom of Kabbalah, which is of "the ancient days", comes to develop whatever is found beyond the five senses of man, and reveals the tremendous forces which are hidden within him. It enlightens the miraculous harmony which exists in the universe and in our world, and directs each person to the harmonious path which is within his own life, and to the harmony which exists between himself and his fellowman.

THE ANSWER TO THE ESSENCE OF LIFE

Kabbalah is the hidden knowledge of Judaism. Kabbalah sees in Judaism an expression of absolute perfection of the universe, not by way of simply relating to the writings of Judaism in their external sense, but by penetrating to the very depth of truth. With the guidance of the book of Zohar written by Rabbi Shimon bar Yochai, it becomes possible for us to reach the essence of things, understand their roots, and directly reveal the solution to problems. Usually man relates to life within the framework of effects and results which are a collection of secondary branches, and which impede man's more basic, primary vision of the complete chain of events. The Kabbalah teaches us to see how the bridges are built between that which is in the Zohar concerning the past, present, and future, and the bridges upon which we have arrived today. The book of Zohar, with an intense light, illuminates the path which leads to the true solution of any problem from the most simple to the most complex.

"There is no question in the universe to which you will not find an answer in the teachings of Kabbalah" Rabbi Dr. P.S. Berg.

COURSES OFFERED IN THE RESEARCH CENTRE OF KABBALAH

It is the privilege of every man to reach the most elevated heights of understanding himself and the universe around him. The way to this understanding is through the teachings of Kabbalah. The Research Centre of Kabbalah presents courses in various fields of Kabbalah and studies in different levels of Zohar ranging from beginners to advanced levels. The following is a list of courses offered in the Research Centre of Kabbalah with a brief description of each course.

* Kabbalah Basic Course

This course includes the definition of terms and an introduction of understanding the principles of Kabbalah. It also includes concepts which are in effect the primary keys to the teaching of mysticism. This course represents an indispensable basis for the rest of the subjects which are taught in the Centre, even to the most advanced levels of Kabbalah studies.

* Kabbalistic Meditation

Kabbalistic meditation is a method of self-reflection dating from ancient days. It is based on the method of the previous Kabbalists and has been unified and simplified by the saintly ARI, Rabbi Yitzhak Luria, one of the great Kabbalists of Safed. This is a practical method which brings us to high levels of awareness and to the true evaluation of the forces which are hidden in man. Kabbalistic meditation acquires for us the tools necessary for bridging the gap between the foces of the soul and the forces of the body, and brings us to a growing utilization of the potential that is imbedded in us.

* Reincarnation and Life After Death

The Kabbalah sees in life not only a process of birth and death, but a continuous chain of cycles in which the soul (the inner energy of man) enters this world to fulfill a particular duty, and "leaves" it several times. The soul returns to the process of life many times in different bodies, up to the point where she reaches a perfect completion of the duty which has been assigned to her.

The understanding of this process leads to the understanding of all the processes which take place in the life of man. During his life time a man may ask himself who he is, why he was born to particular parents in a particular neighborhood; he is called by a name that was "fixed" for him, and finds himself in a particular society to fulfill a particular duty. Why does he meet a particular spouse to bring into the world children with particular personalities and the like? There awaits to be revealed an amazing composition of a picture of a puzzle which when seen explains to us every instant of our lives, and also explains the historical process of life and the world, from its creation to its completion.

"...and in the sixth century of the sixth millenium the gates of wisdom above and the spring of wisdom below will open..." (Zohar, 'Vayera' Part 445).

ADDITIONAL COURSES

*   Kabbalah for the Advanced
This course embraces deeper concepts in the wisdom of the hidden in order to understand the complementing image of the universe in which man is the center.

*   Reincarnation for the Advanced
the technique for discovery of previous incarnation.

*   Kabbalistic Astrology

*   Meditation for the Advanced
The relation between Kabbalistic meditation and Kabbalistic astrology.

*   Essence of Hebrew Letters Their Forces

*   The Week in Zohar
A course that explains the cosmic influence of every week of the year according to the Zohar.

*   Study of the book "Study of the Ten Emanations"

*   Study of the books "Tree of Life" and "Zohar"

*   Kabbalah and Naturalism

*   History of the Kabbalah in Aggadah and in Mysticism

*   The Mystic Aggadah

IS'NT THE KABBALAH STUDY ONLY FOR THOSE OVER 40?

It is commonly heard that the study of Kabbalah is permitted only to people over 40 years of age, and only to individuals who have "filled themselves with the six books of Mishnah and Poskim" and to any other the study of Kabbalah is likely to cause mental and/or emotional imbalance.

This argument is erroneous and in essence has no basis at all. The precise explanation of this argument is as follows: The Kabbalah has two components, "Sitrei Torah" and "Taamei Torah". The study of the "Taamei Torah" deals with the development of inner forces which are imbedded in man and bring him to understanding and seeing the essence of life and the essence of the universe. The study content of the "Taamei Torah" is understandable to every one that desires to study it. While "Sitrei Torah" deals with the secretive studies of the Kabbalah and is reserved only for those who have worked up to the point at which they can sufficiently cope with the forces which are in those secrets.

It is important to understand that the prerequisites of age and spiritual development which are mentioned above relate only to the study of "Sitrei Torah" and there is no prohibition, danger, or doubt whatsoever in regard to the study of "Taamei Torah" in Kabbalah at any age.

The person who has acquired a large and deep knowledge in Kabbalah and is ready to study the secrets of the Torah, in that case will be found by the teacher who will teach him!!!

The Research Centre of Kabbalah is an autonomous and non-profit organization which was established in 1922. Its goal is to publicize the wisdom of Kabbalah and the essence of Judaism to the public at large by way of public lectures, classes, and seminars. The Centre prints and publishes in Hebrew, English, and other languages, ancient and modern Kabbalistic literature, written by the early and later Kabbalists.

Public activities such as spiritual site-seeings, Shabbat and Holy Days gatherings, and seminars on various subjects are organized.

The Centre has several branches in Israel. The main branch is in Tel-Aviv, and publicizes the wisdom of Kabbalah in Jerusalem, Haifa, Safed, Kfar Saba, and also abroad in New York and Los Angeles.

The Centre with all its branches in Israel is open to the public to learn, hear, ask, and become interested in the wisdom of Kabbalah. You are invited to visit any of the branches.

For more information write or call:

THE RESEARCH CENTRE OF KABBALAH

25 Bugrashov Street
Tel-Aviv, ISRAEL 63342
Tel: (03)280-570

200 Park Ave. Suite 303E
New York, N.Y. 10017
Tel: (212)986-2515

Books in English

1 ■ **Kabbalah for the Layman** by Dr. Philip S. Berg.
*The basic concepts of Kabbalah
presented in a simple manner.*

2. ■ **The Kabbalah Connection** by Dr. Philip S. Berg.
A Spiritual Guide to the Cosmic Connection.

3. ■ **An Echo of the Future** by Dr. Philip S. Berg.
A Guide to Kabbalistic Astrology.

4. ■ **The Wheels of a Soul** by Dr. Philip S. Berg.
A Gateway to Kabbalistic Reincarnation.

5. ■ **An Entrance to the Zohar** by Rabbi Yehuda Ashlag.
*A Collection of forward-looking introductions
to the study of Kabbalah.
Edited and compiled by Dr. Philip S. Berg.*

6. ■ **An Entrance to the Tree of Life**
by Rabbi Yehuda Ashlag
Edited and compiled by Dr. Philip S. Berg.

7. ■ **Ten Luminous Emanations (Talmud Eser Sefirot)**
By Rabbi Yehuda Ashlag
*Vol. 1 Interpretation of the Sefirot or Heavenly
Attributes according to the system of Rabbi Yitzhak
Luria. known as the Ari — Edition also contains
Hebrew-to-English text of the Ari's
ETZ CHAIM (TREE OF LIFE).*

8. ■ **Ten Luminous Emanations (Talmud Eser Sefirot)**
by Rabbi Yehuda Ashlag
Vol. II Edited and compiled by Dr. Philip S. Berg.

9. ■ **General Principles of Kabbalah**
by Rabbi Moses Luzzatto
An early 18th Century text in the Lurianic Tradition.

10. ■ **The Light of Redemption**
by Rabbi Levi Krakovski
An introduction to the basic concepts of Kabbalah.

280

11. ■ **Sefer Ha-Zohar — The Book of Splendour**
by Rabbi Shimon Bar Yochai.
English translation — five volumes.

12. ■ **Heaven on Your Head:** by Rabbi S. Z. Kahana
*Esoteric Stories related to mystical experiences
in the Holy Land.*

13. ■ **The Talmud in English:**
*This is a classic in Early Hebrew Education:
Set in 18 Volumes, certainly a library piece.*

14. ■ **Legends of Zion:**
*Tales on this focal point of spiritual energy.
Enlarge your prospectus of great history which occurred
at this place.* Dr. S. Z. Kahana

15. ■ **Legends of Israel:**
*A more broader spectrum of spiritual and esoteric
legend surrounding the Holy Land.* Dr. S. Kahana

16. ■ **Anthology of Jewish Mysicism:**
*Translated from the Hebrew by Raphael Ben Zion.
A different approach to this wonderous teaching.
A fine work even for the uninitiated.*

ספרים בעברית

מס' כרכים

APPENDIX I

Stages of Emanation and Creation

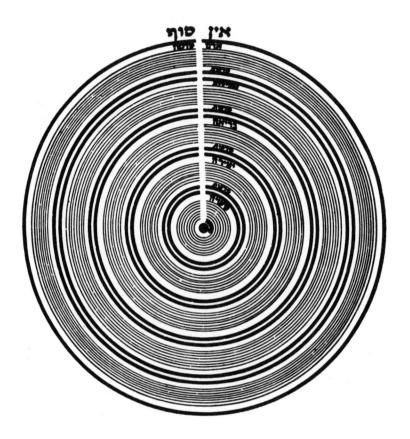

This chart designates that myriads of encircling Sephiroth, like layers of an onion, were gradually revealed in the vacuum, the principle point, Kingdom of the Infinite. The line of light which is issued from the Infinite is breaking through the roofs of all the circles. In general, they are subdivided into five worlds. These are:

1) The world of Adam Kadmon, Crown, from which man's soul derives its top degree of "Yechida."

2) World of Emanation, Wisdom. Man receives from it his spiritual essence of "Chayah."

3) World of Creation, Intelligence from which he gets his "Neshama."

4) World of Formation, Beauty from which "Ruach" is issued to man.

5) World of Action—our world, is the very middle point of the vacuum of Kingdom of the Infinite, Malchut. From this world "Nefesh" is extended to man.

Since Kingdom of the Infinite is the origin to all the worlds, therefore all the circles are connoted by the name of Kingdom, although, the upper circle in relation to its subsequent degrees is called Keter or Crown. Nevertheless, in relation to its origin it is but Kingdom, for Kingdom's last Sephira becomes the Crown to the first world, Adam Kadmon. In other words, the last degree of Kingdom of the Infinite is Kingdom, but in relation to Adam Kadmon it is Crown. The point in the centre is the last Sephira, Kingdom of the world of Action. It is the principal point of the six days, the Sabbath. It is also the heart of man. This is the meaning that every Israelite has a spark of God. It is the spark that he is demanded to sanctify, for its origin stems from the very source of all the sources, the Infinite world. We say it in our Sabbath prayer: "Come let us go to meet the Sabbath, for it is a well-spring of blessing; from the beginning, from of old it was ordained, last in production, first in thought."

APPENDIX II

The Sefirot — Relationship to man

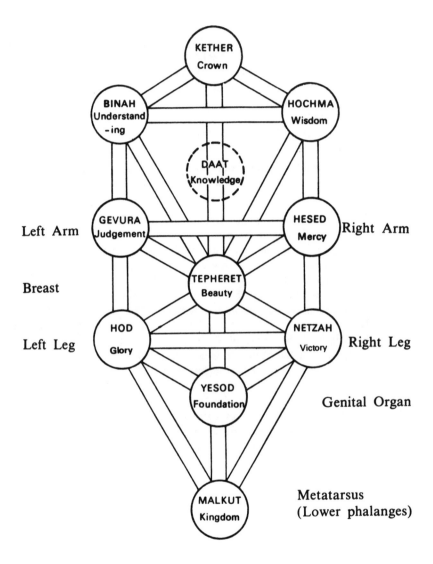

The body tree of man implies the interaction and two-way flow of the various parts of the human body. The complex clearing house is the skull, which assigns messages and cordinates ordinary consciousness.

APPENDIX III

The Sefirot

and

The Twelve Tribes, Months and Astrological Signs

We have learnt that Biblical narrative is the outer covering for many inner levels of concealed truths. An example of this is the story of Jacob and his twelve sons, who became the leaders of the twelve tribes of Israel. The chariot of the bottled-up energy (sefira) of Tiferet contains six sefirot-Hesed, Gevurah, Tiferet, Netzah, Hod, Yesod. Each of these sefirot in its male and female aspect can be attributed to one of the twelve sons, to the twelve months of the year, and to their astrological signs. Of the remaining four sefirot (Keter, Hokhmah, Binah, Malkhut), the upper three have no direct influence on this mundane level of existence, while Malkhut represents the Desire to Receive — Man himself, who is the ultimate recipient of all these energies.

The list below, which is derived from the words of Torah concerning the blessing given by Jacob to his sons, is presented for the reader's interest and information. A more detailed discussion of the subject will be found in a future volume on Astrology and the Kabbalah.

Sefira	Tribe	Months
Hesed	Reuben	Nissan
Gevurah	Shimon	Iyar
Tiferet	Levi	Sivan
Netzah	Yehuda	Tamuz
Hod	Yisechar	Av
Yesod	Zebulun	Elul
Hesed	Binyamin	Tishrei
Gevurah	Dan	Marhesvon
Tiferet	Naftali	Kislev
Netzah	Gad	Tevet
Hod	Asher	Shevat
Yesod	Yosef	Adar

Sign	English	Solar Equivalent
Taleh	Lamb	Aries
Shor	Ox	Taurus
Ti'umin	Twins	Gemini
Sartan	Crab	Cancer
Aryeh	Lion	Leo
Betulah	Virgin	Virgo
Ma'oznaim	Scales	Libra
Akrav	Scorpion	Scorpio
Keshet	Rainbow	Sagittarius
G'di	Goat	Capricorn
D'li	Vessel	Aquarius
Dagim	Fish	Pisces

APPENDIX IV

The Magen David

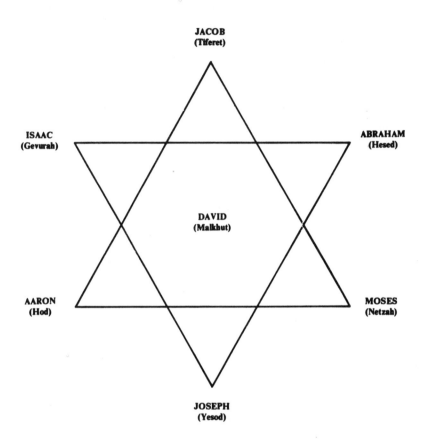

The Shield of David, in a broader sense, implies the concept of cosmic consciousness. When a thorough knowledge of the Upper and Lower Triads has been achieved, then one can reach a Devekut with the cosmos which is represented by the Shield of David. Cosmic influences, namely the seven basic planets together with the twelve signs of the Zodiac are directly related and bound up with the above seven Sefirot. Each Sefirah is considered the internal energy of the seven planets which are as follows: Saturn, Jupiter, Mars, Sun, Venus, Mercury and the Moon in this order. Each planet rules over and dominates two signs of the Zodiac. The sun and moon rule over but one sign. Through Kabbalistic Meditation, one can connect with cosmic consciousness thereby achieving a level of pure awareness. When the individual has mastered the art of direct communion with and an attachment to the interiority of these cosmic influences, the Sefirot, then it is the individual who can now *direct* his destiny.